Leading the Strategically Focused School
Success and Sustainability

Brent Davies

SAGE

Los Angeles • London • New Delhi • Singapore

First Published 2006. Reprinted 2008

SAGE Publications Ltd
1 Oliver's Yard
55 City Road
London EC1Y 1SP

SAGE Publications Inc
2455 Teller Road
Thousand Oaks
California 91320

SAGE Publications India Pvt. Ltd
B 1/I 1 Mohan Cooperative Industrial Area
Mathura Road, New Delhi 110 044
India

SAGE Publications Asia-Pacific Pte Ltd
33 Pekin Street #02-01
Far East Square
Singapore 048763

Library of Congress Control Number: 2005936766

A catalogue record for this book is available from the British Library

ISBN 978-1-4129-1190-0 (hbk)
ISBN 978-1-4129-1191-7 (pbk)

Typeset by Dorwyn Ltd, Wells, Somerset
Printed in Great Britain by Cpod, Trowbridge, Wiltshire
Printed on paper from sustainable resources

This book is dedicated to my strategic intent:
Barbara Jane Davies

Contents

List of figures

Author: Professor Brent Davies,

Cert Ed, BA, MSc, MPhil, PhD

Dr Brent Davies is Professor of International Leadership Development at the University of Hull. He is also a Professorial Fellow at the University of Melbourne, visiting Professor at the Institute of Education London University, a Special Professor at the University of Nottingham and a Faculty Member of the Centre on Educational Governance at the University of Southern California. Brent spent the first ten years of his career working as a teacher in South London. He then moved into higher education and now works exclusively on leadership and management development programmes for senior and middle managers in schools. Brent was Head of Education Leadership at Crewe+Alsager College of Higher Education and then moved to be the Director of the International MBA in School Leadership at Leeds Metropolitan University. He then moved to the University of Lincolnshire and Humberside to establish the first Chair in Educational Leadership and create the International Educational Leadership Centre in Lincoln. He moved to the University of Hull in 2000 to establish the International Leadership Centre. In 2004 he moved within the university to become a research professor in international leadership development at the Hull University Business School.

He has published extensively, with 16 books and 60 articles on leadership and management. His recent books include: *The Essentials of School Leadership* (2005, Sage), *School Leadership in the 21st Century* (2005, Routledge), *The New Strategic Direction and Development of the School* (2003, RoutledgeFalmer) and *The Handbook of Educational Leadership and Management* (2003, Pearson). Brent was co-director and author of the National College of School Leadership (NCSL) research project and report *Success and Sustainability: Developing the Strategically Focused School* (2005, NCSL).

Acknowledgements

I would wish to acknowledge the contribution of countless school leaders who I have worked with over 25 years in the UK, Australia, Hong Kong, New Zealand and the USA on leadership development programmes. They have provided me with the insights and ideas that are included in the book. In particular I would like to thank Linda Ellison with whom I wrote *School Development Planning* (1992), *Strategic Direction and Development of the School* (1999) and *The New Strategic Direction and Development of the School* (2003) for being a strategic colleague in my learning journey. I would like to thank Barbara Davies and Linda Ellison my co-directors on the NCSL research project 'Success and Sustainability: developing the strategically focused school' (2005) for their insights and hard work that produced such a seminal report. I would like to thank Barbara Davies for her leadership model in Chapter 9 which was a conceptual highlight of her doctoral thesis. I put on record my thanks to Martin Coles who at his time at the NCSL supported and developed the research. I thank the NSCL for their help in sponsoring the Success and Sustainability project and for granting permission to replicate the diagrams in Chapters 7 and 8. I thank Sage for permission to use some of the material from my 'Rethinking strategy and strategic leadership in schools', *Educational management and administration*, 2003, 31(3), 295–312; and B. Davies and B.J. Davies (2005) 'Strategic leadership', in B. Davies *Essentials of School Leadership*, London, Paul Chapman Publishing. Thanks must also go to Christopher Bowring-Carr, David Gray and Barbara Davies for proofreading.

Chapter 1

Introduction

We are doing OK now, but I don't think we can keep it up.
We have improved a lot but now we need to do something different.
We are a very good school but that can lead to complacency.
This is a good school but how do we make it a great school?
There must be more to school life than test scores!
I'm always responding to the urgent or the latest initiative.
Do I need to get the basics right before we can look at the strategic?

Why a strategic and sustainable approach is necessary

These are questions and comments articulated to me by school leaders during 25 years of running seminars, workshops and undertaking research. The drive to raise educational standards has, over the past decade, concentrated on more tightly focused curricular frameworks and testing regimes. This focus has undoubtedly raised standards as measured by test scores. However, it raises two questions: 'Are these scores meaningful?' and 'Are they sustainable?'

Achieving success for children in terms of how they develop academically, socially, physically and spiritually is the aim of all schools. How do we achieve that success both in the short term and long term? How do we ensure that success is sustainable? It is important to understand sustainability not as a continuation of the status quo but as sustainable improvement. Sustainability might be considered as the ability of schools to continue to adapt and improve to meet new challenges and be successful in new and demanding contexts. This sustainability should be seen in the context of improving, not depleting, individual and organizational health and well-being. The challenge is that the short-term and the long-term agendas should be compatible and not contradictory.

The ability both to manage the current situation and provide strategic leadership for the future can be seen in examples provided by both primary and secondary schools. For example, in a primary school the need is to provide a child entering nursery with a variety of learning opportunities for her to develop during this year, while at the same time rising to the challenge of developing an understanding of what a successful learning environment will need to provide for that child in six or seven years' time when she is in year 6. The school will also need to pay attention to ensuring that those who work in the school enhance their skills and abilities necessary to meet the challenges of a rapidly changing environment. Similarly, a parent whose son has successfully completed secondary school and whose daughter is about to start might say: 'My son had a great experience; just give the same experience to my daughter.' The challenge for the school is to reflect on the best of the previous approach while at the time seeking to provide an education that in seven years' time will provide the abilities and skills for the daughter to engage in a rapidly changing world.

How can schools plan to be effective now and in the future? In the business world, two of the most influential books in the first decade of the twenty-first century have been Jim Collins's *Good to Great* (2001) and Robert Kaplan and David Norton's *The Strategy-Focused Organization* (2001). Collins led a major research project over five years looking at 1,435 companies to determine features of companies that allowed them to move from being 'good' in their historical contexts to being outstanding companies in the present day. He isolates the factors that made them strategically effective and leaders in their field in the longer term. Kaplan and Norton use the results of ten years of research in deploying their 'Balanced Scorecard' approach to demonstrate how organizations can both design and deploy effective strategic approaches to sustain development over the longer term. In the educational world there is similar interest in the factors that contribute to longer-term success as witnessed by Michael Fullan in his *Leadership and Sustainability* (2004), in which he articulates how schools can build sustainable longer-term development. Andy Hargreaves and Dean Fink (2005) join this emerging literature in their book *Sustaining Leadership*, which seeks to provide insights into the challenge of moving away from short-term results-driven agendas, to sustainable longer-term educational development. Davies (2007) brings together ten leading authors to further develop the concept of sustainability. All these authors provide a commentary on how organizations can build longer-term sustainable development.

This book provides insights on how schools can build longer-term success and sustainability by developing strategic capability and capacity to become a strategically focused school, which can be defined as:

> *A strategically focused school is one that is educationally effective in the short term but has a clear framework and processes to translate core moral purpose and vision into excellent educational provision that is challenging and sustainable in the medium- to long-term.*

The book does not take a traditional view of strategy in terms of those at the top of an organization undertaking a strategic planning exercise using a number of mechanistic techniques. It is about all those who work in school both understanding how to do the day-to-day tactical activities such as planning lessons, organizing schedules and timetables, and dealing with student behaviour, *but* also stepping outside the box and being aware of the bigger issues such as the developments in learning and how they impact on the school, and the increasing impact of technology and its impact on the role of the teacher. It is about providing a way of doing the 'now' and concurrently addressing what should and could be.

Developing strategic thinking as well as operational competence is an ability that we should develop in all staff in a school. Strategic thinking is not necessarily aligned to an individual's role in the school's hierarchy, nor does strategy necessarily come at a stage when the management process has been mastered. I believe, from my research, that leaders in schools, classroom leaders, and subject co-ordinators or faculty leaders, as well as deputy headteachers and headteachers, can operate in two modes concurrently. They can choose to undertake a current task but also see how that task is part of a larger strategic educational picture. To me, how we distinguish between administration/management and leadership is how individuals both operate in the 'now' of the current school year, while challenging and creating new ways of doing things for the future. We need to develop leaders in our school who can have a vision but also translate that vision into action.

This book explores a model of strategy which comprises the *strategic processes* that schools can engage in to develop capacity for strategic development, *strategic approaches* they can deploy to enact the strategy and *strategic leadership* which is necessary to drive and facilitate the whole-school development. The aim of the three-element model is to provide a framework for sustainable long-term success.

This book draws on my work with a large number of headteachers and their staff over the past 25 years in the UK and overseas, and insights gained from the National College for School Leadership (NCSL) research project, 'Success and Sustainability: developing the strategically focused school'. This has provided me with a number of 'leadership voices' which I have included in the text to link ideas and practice together. I would like to pay tribute to the work of my colleagues Barbara Davies and Linda Ellison who worked with me on the project and to Martin Coles, who was at that time at the NCSL, for his expert guidance and support.

One of the frequent sayings from my childhood is 'hard work never killed anyone'. Experience has taught me that excessive hard work does! What we need to do in schools is move away from adding additional activities and from a steadily increasing workload, and to stand back and look at the bigger picture. By defining the strategic context and prioritizing activities there is the possibility of concentrating activity and working in a more effective way.

Key questions

In the following chapters, the book aims to answer the following questions:

- What is meant by leading for sustainable strategic success?
- What does a school mean by values and beliefs?
- What are strategic processes?
- What are strategic approaches?
- What is strategic leadership?
- What is an effective strategic implementation?
- What do strategically focused schools look like?

This set of questions provides the framework for the following chapters, as outlined in Figure 1.1.

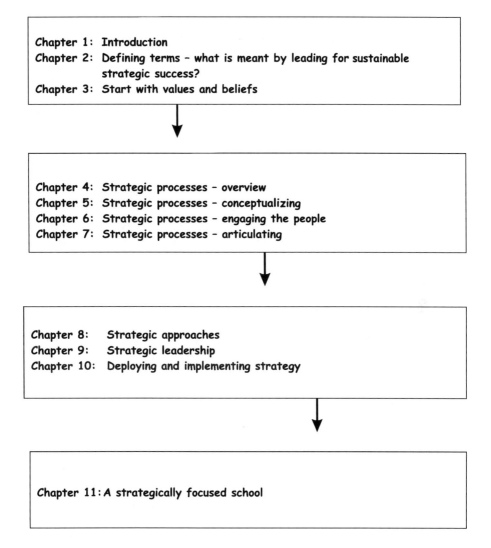

Figure 1.1 *Chapter schematic*

In Chapter 2, the book starts to define what we understand by leading for sustainable strategic success. This chapter explores the nature of leading a strategic and sustainable approach as a means of delivering success in the medium to long term. It undertakes initial definitions of strategy, success, sustainability and leadership, as a means of building a common understanding and language for ideas and proposals in the rest of the book. It then moves on to explore a model that will help schools form a coherent and deliverable strategic framework for their actions. The model (shown in Figure 2.4) links strategic processes, strategic approaches and strategic leadership in a dynamic interrelated way to develop strategic capacity and capability in the school.

Chapter 3 argues that the essential first stage for schools, before they move into strategic development, is to clarify and clearly articulate the school's values and beliefs. This stage is based on the view that strategy should not exist in a vacuum; it must be based on a set of values and beliefs. When difficult choices have to be made, it is vital that alternatives are set against how well they fulfil the school's values. Similarly, when one looks at the values that the school articulates, they should not just be something that the school articulates for the external world but those values must infuse the whole school's working practices, including the strategic development process itself. Setting these values in place, and reviewing and updating them is the critical first stage in the development of a strategically focused school.

In Chapter 4, the book articulates the model employed in defining strategic processes. Processes are *the* critical factor in making strategy a reality and a force for real change in schools. There are a number of leadership and management maxims which are useful to consider here. For example, *how* we undertake something is equally import as *what* we undertake in building long-term success. This idea draws attention to the process of building strategic capability and leads to the maxim of 'process is policy'. This latter statement suggests that policy is not formed and then implemented, but that it is the interaction of the evolving process and the people involved that forms the policy. The 'how' of strategic processes can be divided into three elements that build a strategic direction and activity for the school. These process elements are conceptualization, engaging people and articulation.

Chapter 5 considers how the *conceptualization* element focuses on the processes of reflection, strategic thinking, analysis and creating new ways of understanding, by creating mental models of the new reality. Chapter 6 suggests that the *engaging people* part of the process starts with a critical review of the importance of strategic conversations, to facilitate increased strategic participation which, in turn, leads to enhanced levels of motivation and builds strategic capability. Chapter 7 looks at the *articulation* part of the three process elements and highlights oral, written and structural means of communicating and developing strategic purpose.

Chapter 8 examines the strategic approaches a school can utilize and deploy. It considers four approaches. Initially it looks at the proactive and rational linear approach of *strategic* planning, which is the traditional approach to strategy. It assumes that the school understands the goals it wishes to achieve, how to measure the outcomes and how to plan the journey to achieve those outcomes. The methodology of this traditional approach underpins much of the school development and school improvement literature. It then contrasts this approach with the reactive approach of *emergent strategy*, which is a means of harnessing current experience to formulate future strategy, as seen in situations where schools 'learn by doing'. Patterns of success and failure emerge if the school is a reflective and learning organization and the school will repeat the successes and not repeat the failures. Thus a pattern of strategic actions emerges from experience, which can be welded together in a more coherent strategic framework. Emergent strategy can be considered to be a reflective and reactive process initially, which draws on experience to build future patterns of behaviour. The chapter looks next at the role of *decentralized strategy* as a model of strategic development. Decentralized strategy is seen when senior leaders outline key directions and outcomes for the school, but delegate the details of implementation and policy to other staff in the school. This is dependent as an approach on clear values and a high level of trust between the various partners in the school. Finally, Chapter 8 looks at the powerful approach of *strategic intent* as a means of building capability and capacity to leverage significant strategic change. Strategic intent is a means of setting clear objectives (intents) that the organization is committed to achieving, but recognizing that it is necessary to build capability and capacity to fully understand how and when they can be achieved. This is a combined process of strategic direction and strategic learning.

Chapter 9 looks at building and sustaining strategic leadership within the school as the key to driving the strategic processes and approaches to successful outcomes. The chapter examines what strategic leaders do in terms of direction setting, translating strategy into action, aligning people and the organization to the strategy, determining effective intervention points and developing strategic capabilities within the school. The chapter then moves on to consider the characteristics which strategic leaders display and whether these can be developed in others. It focuses on characteristics of strategic leaders, such as: they challenge and question; they have a dissatisfaction or restlessness with the present; they prioritize their own strategic thinking and learning; they build new mental models to frame their own and others' understanding; they display strategic wisdom based on a clear value system; they have powerful personal and professional networks, they have high-quality personal and interpersonal skills and display emotional intelligence (EQ).

Chapter 10 considers the challenge of *implementing* policy. The chapter focuses on the challenges of translating strategy into action and the key elements of strategic timing and abandonment. Mintzberg (2003: 79–84) uses a definition of strategy as 'seeing', such as seeing ahead; perceptively, he also uses strategy as 'seeing it through'. Many schools have elaborate plans but how many of them get significantly implemented? Davies and Ellison (2003) use the saying 'the thicker the plan the less it effects practice'. Attention needs to be paid not only to developing the strategy but also its implementation, so that it successfully focuses the school's activities.

Chapter 11, the final chapter, explores the characteristics of successful strategically focused schools. It draws together nine themes that contribute to building strategically focused schools. It suggests that strategically focused schools should:

1. develop a culture of sustainability;
2. balance short term and long term;
3. develop strategic measures of success;
4. be morally driven;
5. focus on learning: children – adults – learning for reflection and improvement;
6. pay attention to strategic processes;
7. pay attention to strategic approaches;
8. be part of networked systems; and
9. develop strategic leadership across the school that is sustainable.

Throughout the book, use is made of the 'leadership voices' of headteachers from the NCSL research study to articulate key ideas. Suggestions are made to share good practice from the research. The purpose of this book is to encourage all those who work in schools, and those who work with schools, to move beyond the Office for Standards in Education (Ofsted) inspection approach of planning through short-term targets, in order to set those plans within a strategic framework.

While I, and other educationalists, recognize the value of short-term planning, I believe such planning can be effective only if it is set within a more holistic planning framework. To that end, this book provides a means of examining how a school might build on its current school improvement or school development planning, by building a strategic dimension. I see this dimension as a strategic framework that will include a written element but, more importantly, will include strategic processes and approaches to involve the staff in defining how the school is developing and where the school is going.

Two of the challenges facing all school leaders are summed up by Hamel and Prahalad (1994):

So the urgent drives out the important; the future goes largely unexplored; and the capacity to act, rather than the capacity to think and imagine becomes the sole measure for leadership. (Hamel and Prahalad, 1994: 4–5)

and by Charles Handy:

We are all prisoners of our past. It is hard to think of things except in the way we have always thought of them. But that solves no problems and seldom changes anything. (Handy, 1990: 54)

How do we move beyond simply responding or reacting to the urgent? To think differently, to create an improved future for the school, involves building a strategic framework for a school. How to establish that framework to enable a strategic dialogue to take place forms the structure and contents of the rest of this book.

Chapter 2

What is meant by leading for sustainable strategic success?

When facing strong winds, some build walls to protect themselves; others construct windmills (Chinese proverb)

Why be a strategic and sustainable school?

The proverb suggests that hiding behind the wall may be a solution to the future, but a more sustainable solution and a more strategic approach may be one of providing sustainable energy! How can we be more strategic and more successful? This chapter seeks to establish a framework for strategic success and sustainability. In doing so it is useful initially to develop the definition of a strategically successful school given in Chapter 1, by integrating the leadership dimension as follows:

A strategically focused school is one that is educationally effective in the short term but also has a clear framework and processes to translate core moral purpose and vision into excellent educational provision that is challenging and sustainable in the medium to long term. It has the leadership that enables short-term objectives to be met while concurrently building capability and capacity for the long term.

To consider how the book defines success, sustainability, strategy and leadership I will now take each of these concepts in turn.

Success

Success can be seen in how children achieve academically, socially, spiritually, physically and emotionally; it is enabling children to be all they can be. The difficult question is how do you know that you have been successful? Standardized test scores, even when adjusted for value-added dimensions, tell only part of the story. Two challenges emerge. One is that measuring success by easily quantifiable measures is to ignore that some aspects of success are recognized by indicators which point to success, but do not by any means fully explain or measure that success. Secondly, approaches that make schools successful initially may not be the ones that are necessary to take them on to higher levels of performance, so that isolating what approaches lead to sustainable success is difficult. A good example of this is the difference between shallow and deep learning. Coaching children for standard assessment tasks (SATs) tests may increase short-term results and the school would be considered successful. However, instead of putting in enormous effort every year to boost results, a longer-term and more sustainable approach would be to involve 'deep learning' approaches that develop a learning culture in individuals and the school. Thus, coming out of a difficult period, a school may decide politically that it needs to raise short-term results but it will have to change its long-term approach if children and teachers are not to 'burn out' by knowledge replication rather than knowledge understanding.

Using valued-added data, the Hay Group (Hay Group Education, 2004) looked at the school culture that led to success in terms of sustainable improvement. The high improvement schools had a demanding culture and focused on raising capability, promoting excellence, making sacrifices to put pupils first and concentrating on value-added measures. A characteristic of these high improvement schools is the development of a culture based on the view that every child can improve and working together to learn more effectively is a way to achieve that. The schools that were less successful in that their value-added results were more focused on keeping up with initiatives, doing what was required, creating a pleasant working environment and making allowances for underperformance. This is not just about being good at the task and being good with people. It is more about giving a sharper focus to the factors that directly impact on children's learning and achievement.

Perkins (2003) talks about being 'process smart' and 'people smart', where success is achieved by a series of progressive interactions that move the organization forward and by a cohesive working environment that encourages people to work together. This approach leads on to a consideration of sustainability. Later I will discuss the difference between operational and strategic measures of success in more detail. A basic consideration now would be to draw a distinction between how the school had been judged to be successful by its short-term results and what might be considered to be strategic success. While the former may use assessment results or attendance rates, the latter might pose questions such as 'What would a strategically focused school look like?' It may be that a strategic measure of success would be more staff staying on at the end of the day to discuss the learning and teaching challenges they had faced or sharing insights with colleagues. Other measures of success could be considered to be improved attitudes to learning and involvement in wider curricular issues and events by students. A key success measure might be staff recommending colleagues to work at the school or sending their own children there. Certainly a success culture would be based on children achieving their personal best and the school always accentuating the positive. It is important to see success not just as measured by test and examination results but as a wider set of features that encompass the school's values and the way individuals live out those values in their day-to-day interactions.

Sustainability

Sustainability is not the same as maintainability! Nor does it simply mean whether something can last. Success is challenging to articulate and difficult to embed but even more difficult to sustain. Sustainability may be considered as building on the past but also leaping forward to new ways of learning and organizational performance, in a way that enhances organizational and human resources and does not deplete or demoralize them. It is about nourishing and developing organizations. Fullan (2004: 22) states:

Sustainability by our definition requires continuous improvement, adaptation, and collective problem solving in the face of complex challenges that keep arising.

Hargreaves and Fink (2005: 5) argue:

the environmental movement and its commitment to sustainability, teaches vital lessons for achieving sustainability in educational and other organizations too: the value of rich diversity over soulless standardization, the necessity of taking the long view, the wisdom of being prudent about conserving and renewing human resources, the moral obligation to consider the effect our improvement efforts have on others in the environment around us, the importance of acting urgently for change while waiting patiently for results.

When we consider these definitions of sustainability to build our own understanding it is useful to relate the concept of sustainability to: the individuals within the school such as staff and pupils; groups of individuals such as particular class/year groups and different staff groupings; the school as an organization; and, finally, the wider community that supports and surrounds the school. The sustainability context is how to provide challenge without exhausting the individual or the group, how to renew and rebuild individuals and the organization, how to achieve short-term success without sacrificing longer-term goodwill and individual or organizational ability and capacity. A degree of organizational challenge and stress is a motivation to action, but too much damages individuals and organizational capacity. As an extension to my earlier ideas about sustainability, a useful definition might be:

the ability of individuals and schools to continue to improve to meet new challenges and complexity in a way that does not damage individuals or the wider community but builds capacity and capability to be successful in new and demanding contexts.

This book seeks an approach where short-term and long-term aims are built together. There are two threats to this way of thinking. One is that schools use sequential thinking and approaches; by that I mean they deal with short-term issues and agendas first and then move on to the more strategic longer-term issues. This sequence can result in taking action on issues in isolation from the longer-term implications of those actions. As Pfeffer and Sutton (2002) argue, the tyranny of short-term targets can also lead to the neglect of the longer term. Secondly, fear of failure with short-term agendas and issues can lead individuals to protect their own interests rather than promoting collaborative collective interests and longer-term viability. I shall argue later in this book (Chapter 9) that strategic leaders operate a parallel approach by concurrently striving to improve current performance, while at the same time building longer-term strategic capability. While it is important to run this parallel approach, the essence of doing this is that the process is integrated so that what happens in the short term contributes to and supports longer-term activities. By doing so, resources, and especially people, are effectively deployed and staff are motivated and enhanced in their abilities, and not exhausted and demotivated by the time they get to the long run.

Strategy

Strategy involves linking a number of ideas or concepts. The first is that it involves a series of actions either consciously taken or reacted to, so that it shapes the *direction of the organization*. This future, forward-looking element of where the school is going was articulated by the leaders in the NCSL study as:

> *Strategy is about having a plan of where you are going and why you are going.*

> *Your strategy is how you are going to get there, what kind of structures you put in place in the school, what measures you take to make things happen, how you use the money – all these things build up a strategy to getting where you want to get to.*

In a school setting I would see this as *a medium- to longer-term activity*, say a three- to five-year view and beyond. Leaders in the NCSL study commented:

> *Strategy for me is taking a long-term view about how to make realistic sense of the vision and how you achieve that vision over a period of time. At the moment we are working with a five-year timescale and I think that is right for a strategic plan*

> *Strategy is a more medium-term realistic step towards a vision. School development planning is a fairly short-term operation for specific events and activities.*

Strategy also involves taking a view of *broader core issues* and themes for developments in the school, rather than the detail of day-to-day imperatives. This approach was seen by leaders in the study as:

> *I think when we talk about strategy within the school that we are actually talking about the main features of the school, how they develop and how we adapt to changing issues and challenges. We are seeing which are appropriate or not and how they fit with our direction in school.*

> *To me strategy is the way of me trying to look forward to make sense of a whole big picture and find ways of going forward and improving my school in a number of ways.*

It may be useful initially to think of strategy as aligned to *strategic thinking* and a *strategic perspective* rather that just the traditional view of strategy being linked to mechanistic strategic plans. Unfortunately strategy has become synonymous with strategic planning, which is a mistake since strategy is a much wider concept. It may be useful to think of strategy more as a perspective, a way of thinking about things. Garratt (2003: 2–3) gives an excellent definition of strategic thinking:

> *Strategic thinking is the process by which an organization's direction-givers can rise above the daily managerial processes and crises to gain different perspectives ... Such perspectives should be both future-oriented and historically understood. Strategic thinkers must have the skills of looking ... forwards ... while knowing where their organization is now, so that wise risks can be taken while avoiding having to repeat the mistakes of the past.*

This definition by Garratt highlights two factors: first, standing above the day-to-day operational issues and looking at the bigger picture; second, understanding strategy both in terms of where you have been as well as where you are going. This seeing where you have come from as well as where you are going is taken up by Mintzberg. Mintzberg (2003: 79–83) gives a famous definition of strategic thinking as 'seeing'. This involves seeing where you are going (seeing ahead) as well as seeing where you have come from (seeing behind) and, most significantly, 'seeing it through' to make sure strategy is turned into action. In essence, strategy is the way that we look at the school in the broader context of its current situation and its future direction with the skills necessary to implement successfully any actions.

It is useful to think of strategy as a *framework* to set future direction and action, and as a *template* against which to judge current activities. This idea of a template is a significant one. The ability to align short-term actions in the school development plan (SDP) with long-term strategic objectives is a means of ensuring that strategy is integrated into the school's practice and is not seen as a bolt-on activity. Also, as a template or framework, a set of strategies can be used to evaluate a series of much shorter-term activities to see if they contribute to the much larger plan. These strategic benchmarks or direction points were articulated by leaders in the NCSL study as:

> *What I find helps me is to have some key strategic direction points that I can keep referring to. It is very easy to get diverted by current challenges and forget about what is really important and what you are trying to achieve in the longer term. What I need is a set of compass points that I can keep coming back to.*

> *The staff and I have a set of strategic benchmarks for what we are trying to achieve over the next five years. What is really important to us and why it is important is a key issue. We then use those benchmarks as a framework for current decisions. We ask ourselves will undertaking a certain activity help us achieve those strategic benchmarks or not? It is important for us to keep focused.*

Finally, strategy is about providing for the *sustainability* of the school. Strategy is not isolated from shorter-term planning but integrated with it. It needs to be built on sound short-term operational planning, and vice versa. Obviously it is important that improving schools do not regress to previous underperformance and that successful schools can build on that success and move to significantly higher levels of performance. To achieve this, schools not only need short-term improvement agendas but also a strategic approach to longer-term sustainability. This is represented in Figure 2.1. Short-term effectiveness will not be sustainable if longer-term strategic approaches are not established. Schools will not be able to deploy longer-term strategy if short-term ineffectiveness drives the school into crises. The ideal therefore is to ensure that shorter-term effectiveness is complemented with a longer-term effective strategy.

			Ineffective	Effective
Operational processes and planning (SDP and target setting)	**Effective**		Functionally successful in the short term but not sustainable long term	Successful and sustainable in both the short term and long term
	Ineffective		Failure inevitable both in the short and long term	Short-term crises will prevent longer-term sustainability
			Ineffective	**Effective**
			Strategic processes and approaches	

Figure 2.1 *Short-term viability and long-term sustainability (based on Davies, B.J., 2004)*

This was expressed very succinctly by one of the leaders in the study:

It is a dual approach really – how to get the staff to give the best deal possible to the kids today but to get them to rethink the way it might be a different deal in the future!

The way that strategy works can be seen in the model of strategic development where schools develop a series of *strategic processes* that can ensure the effective development and deployment of strategy through the use of appropriate *strategic approaches*. This is brought together by strategic leadership, which we will consider next.

Leadership – strategic leadership – sustainable leadership

Leadership

Strategy encompasses direction setting, broad aggregated agendas, a perspective to view the future and a template against which to evaluate current activities. Leadership is defined by Bush and Glover (2003: 8) as:

> *a process of influence leading to the achievement of desired purposes. It involves inspiring and supporting others towards the achievement of a vision for the school which is based on clear personal and professional values.*

This is a good initial definition of leadership. It is next necessary to explore the difference between leadership and management. Leadership can be seen more as direction setting and management is more concerned with effectively dealing with the current shape of the organization. Bennis and Nanus (1985: 20) provide a classic definition of the difference:

> *The problem with many organizations ... is that they tend to be over managed and under led. They may excel in the ability to handle the daily routine, yet never question whether the routine should be done at all. There is a profound difference between management and leadership, and both are important. 'To manage' means 'to bring about, to accomplish to have charge of or responsibility for, to conduct.' 'Leading' is 'influencing, guiding in direction, course, action, opinion.' The distinction is crucial. Managers are people who do things right and leaders are people who do the right things. The differences may be summarized as activities of vision and judgement – effectiveness versus activities of mastering routines – efficiently.*

Building on these definitions of leadership it is now possible to link in the strategic element of leadership. Strategic leaders are concerned with not just managing the now but setting up a framework of where the organization needs to be in the future, setting a direction for the organization. The position of strategic leadership is driving the visioning process of moral purpose and future direction while maintaining the day-to-day operation of a school.

Strategic leadership

School leaders articulate the definition of the organization's moral purpose, which can be considered as 'why we do what we do' and, significantly, 'why we do not do what we do not do'. The values that underpin this moral purpose are linked to the vision considering 'where we want to be and what sort of organization we want to be in the future'. Strategic leadership is the means of linking this broad activity to shorter-term operational planning, thereby imbuing the responses to immediate events with elements of the value system and the longer-term strategic direction. This is represented diagrammatically in Figure 2.2.

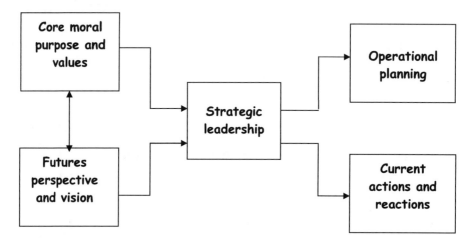

Figure 2.2 *The linking role of strategic leadership*

Strategic leadership therefore defines and translates the vision and moral purpose into action. It is a delivery mechanism for building the direction and the capacity for the organization to achieve that directional shift or change. This translation requires a proactive transformational mind-set which strives for something better, rather than the maintenance approach of transactional leadership.

Sustainable leadership

Here we can make use of the ideas of two influential writers in the field. Jim Collins and George Porras (1994) in their book *Built to Last* look at firms that have been strategically successful over a long period of time and highlight six factors from the successful firms:

- putting pupose before short-term results;
- start slowly; advance persistently;

- do not depend on a single visionary leader;
- grow their own leadership instead of importing 'stars';
- learn from diverse experimentation (Collins and Porras, 1994: 2).

They compare 18 companies that have been successful over the longer term with 18 companies that have been less successful. They identify what has made the success of the 'good' firms sustainable over the longer term. The leadership of these organizations used an approach that made the firms both successful and sustainable.

Jim Collins (2001) builds on this work in his book *Good to Great*. In this book he identifies that levels of leadership work through five stages: highly capable individual, contributing team member, competent manager, effective leader and executive. The challenge is to move from level 4 leaders who are highly effective but see themselves as the sole factor in success and see the 'I' of achievement as more important than the 'we' of the organization. They often leave the organization without effective leaders to succeed them. Level 5 leaders 'channel their ego needs away from themselves and into the larger goal of building a great company. It's not that Level 5 leaders have no ego or self-interest. Indeed, they are incredibly ambitious – but their ambition is first and foremost for the institution, not for themselves' (Collins, 2001: 21) Collins summarizes two sides of leaders who have been successful in the long term as those of professional will and the personal quality of humility that goes with it. He demonstrates the dimensions of this categories in Figure 2.3.

Professional will	Personal humility
Creates superb results, a clear catalyst in the transition from good to great.	Demonstrates a compelling modesty, shunning public adulation; never boastful.
Demonstrates an unwavering resolve to do whatever must be done to produce the best long-term results, no matter how difficult.	Acts with quiet calm determination; relies principally on inspired standards, not inspiring charisma, to motivate.
Sets the standard of building an enduring great company; will settle for nothing less.	Channels ambition into the company, not the self; sets up successors for even greater success in the next generation.

Figure 2.3 *Characteristics of successful leaders (Collins, 2001: 36)*

This links back to the 'process smart' and 'people smart' discussion earlier. Building long-term capacity and capability is what strategy is all about, and making that achievement not just a one-off event but linked to sustainable processes connects strategy and sustainability together by developing sustainable leadership.

Hargreaves (2005) develops the idea of leaders and sustainability within an educational context. He makes a passionate case for not just achieving long-term desirable goals but doing so in a way that is both desirable and supportable.

> *In summary, leaders develop sustainability by how they approach, commit to and protect deep learning in their schools; by how they sustain themselves and others around them to promote and support that learning; by how they are able and encouraged to sustain themselves in doing so, so that they can persist with their vision and avoid burning out; by how they try to ensure the improvements they bring last over time, especially after they themselves have gone; and by how they promote and perpetuate ... diversity rather than standardized prescription in teaching and learning within their schools. Sustainable leadership often defers gratification, respects the past, scans and monitors the environment, and engages with it in an urgent and activist way.*
> *(Hargreaves, 2005: 187)*

I would consider that sustainable leadership is by definition strategic leadership in its nature. How would we recognize a strategically focused school that is trying to build sustainable capacity? The following case example which has been researched over the past six years provides an example of short-term and longer-term sustainable approaches.

Case example – one school, two leaders

This is a case study undertaken over a six-year period at one school in the South East of England where one leader 'Peter' served as headteacher for three years and then was succeeded by 'Jane'.

The school had been apparently successful having good SATs results and a good Ofsted report. It had been led by Peter, a confident man who was outstanding at promoting the school (and himself) in the local community. However, after continual battles with the governing body and staff, Peter leaves and Jane takes over the headship. What is the reality on the ground?

Peter

It is clear that for Peter, targets and SATs results are all-important and he continually forces teachers to adopt shallow learning approaches to enable children to replicate facts in official government tests. He is a very articulate individual, good at promoting himself. He was very successful in persuading the last Ofsted inspection team that the schools' test results were a good measure of how good the school was. Staff, while appreciating the importance of the testing regime, are increasingly demoralized by the approaches being advocated by Peter. Achievements are hyped up, especially of the boy's football team where the 'few' team members are singled out for praise while the 'many' (including all the girls!) receive little attention. Marketing is based on test results and achievements in sport, which are both good. Peter is especially good at promoting himself at large publicity meetings but rarely attends the reporting to parents' evenings. In terms of leadership as outlined by Collins (2001) this would equate to level 3 or 4 leadership where the 'I' of leadership is paramount; everything is seen in terms of how it affects the individual leader.

There are alternative cultures being set up in the school by teachers who seek to protect themselves. One such culture is seen in which staff undertake a number of compliance activities that fulfil the requirements of the headteacher. The other, is where they work among themselves in small groups to build learning and teaching cultures that they are confident with and they believe promote 'deep learning' for pupils. The staff feel things are 'done to them' and often feel 'done in' (Novak, 2002), and are increasingly withdrawing into their own classrooms. There is an increasing compliance with the wishes of Peter rather than a broader professional debate. There is little articulation of the values of the school and the ethical basis on which individuals relate to each other. Planning is short term, run by the headteacher alone and focused on one-year targets. He writes a one-year school development plan by himself. He has also written the school policies copied from a Department for Education and Skills (DfES) website. There is no policy for learning.

Peter is involved in educational consultancy and has a reputation for not always being in the school. He is not involved in classrooms and does little in the way of mentoring or coaching staff. Some teachers have involved their trade union in complaints against the headteacher.

Governors are increasingly at 'loggerheads' with Peter and relation-ships have deteriorated considerably. However, through the external inspection system, the school is judged to be successful.

Jane

Jane took over the school, after considerable previous experience in headship. While recognizing the need to deliver short-term results she believes far more in developing meaningful learning through an inte-grated curricular approach with highly engaged staff. With a clear per-sonal and professional educational value system, she possesses a quiet determination but is not a natural 'marketer' and does not 'sell' herself at the expense of the staff team or the school. She believes in distrib-uted leadership and seeks to build a learning community of staff and pupils. In terms of Collins's levels of leadership she could be catego-rized as a level 5 leader – seeking success for the school and not per-sonalized success for herself. In a sense this could be characterized as quiet leadership.

By refocusing the school on learning and adopting different learning approaches, she aims to meet short-term targets by the quality of the children's experience being reflected in their achievements and those demonstrated in the outcome measures. These targets are achieved by reculturing the staff into a high-achievement culture that focuses on the individual child's learning needs. Her philosophy is one of working with the staff so that the culture is one of 'done with' rather than 'done to'. This applies to values of inclusion, collaboration and improving on personal best. She sets out a way of working together based on honesty and integrity as well as transparency as a means of building a profes-sional dialogue within the school.

Although clearly a people person, Jane's main challenge has been to break the school out of a culture of complacency and move it to one of high achievement by challenging performance to achieve excellence. This change has involved a slow process of building professional accountability for children's learning and challenging previous assumptions and attitudes to learning. She has a clear strategic vision for the school and has both the patience and the determination to achieve it.

Compared with Peter she is far more in evidence in the classroom, working with teachers and monitoring standards, and involving the leadership team in taking greater responsibilities for colleagues' teaching and learning approaches. She is particularly committed to developing strategic and future plans to run alongside the mandatory short-term school improvement plan.

Implications of the case study

While the names of the leaders have been changed, the reality of the case study points up the significance of building longer-term strategic capacity in schools. In terms of Collins's (2001) dimensions of professional will and personal humility, it is clear that one head (Jane) is far more likely to reflect these and put the school on a successful path that is sustainable both in the long and short terms. Major foci of setting the longer-term context, building strategic plans and leading with moral and ethical behaviour are key attributes of strategic leadership. Also very significant are the people dimensions of Jane's leadership style, of involving colleagues and building the capacity to work together, with a set of sustainable relationships. Making judgements about success you would probably say in the short term both leaders were successful but there is considerable doubt whether the leadership style of Peter, lacking a people and a strategic focus, had any sustainable characteristics.

Strategic leadership is sustainable and builds capacity to meet the challenges of the longer term as well as dealing with the day-to-day challenges of the organization. It is based on values and seeks to sustain deep learning and improvement.

Building a framework for leading a strategically focused school for success and sustainability

How can Jane reflect on whether she is on the right track and how can readers of this book reflect on what are the critical factors in building a sustainable and strategic framework for her school? I suggest that success and sustainability can be achieved by considering a model for leading a successful strategically focused school as shown in Figure 2.4.

The book examines each of the main components of the model. In Chapters 4 to 7 it will consider how schools build strategic processes that involve all those in the school community in achieving a future direction for the school. In Chapter 8 it considers how those processes can work through different strategic approaches as a means of developing strategy. Then in Chapter 9 it reviews the nature of strategic leadership. However, all these strategic processes, approaches and leadership must be underpinned by a clear value and belief system and that is considered first, in Chapter 3.

Figure 2.4 *Elements contributing to the strategically focused school*

Chapter 3

Start with values and beliefs

It is important that the strategy process is not seen just as a functional means of moving the school from one stage in its development to the next. The strategy process needs to be based on a series of values and beliefs that aim to improve the lives of children and those who work in the school. Usually we think of having a vision for the school which is based on a set of core values and beliefs.

We need to be careful in our use of terms in this area. I see futures and strategic thinking as a way of building an overall perspective of where we are going, and strategic processes and approaches as the means of reaching that destination. Vision is an overarching concept which is both emotional and rational. It is emotional in that it inspires and reaches the heart of human experience, and it is rational in that it defines what is achievable. Visions can be moral or immoral. To be moral, visions need to be based on a set of values and beliefs. First, we will look briefly at the concept of vision and then move on to consider values and beliefs.

Vision

A valuable and useful definition of vision is provided by Nanus (1992: 8), 'a vision is a realistic, credible, attractive future for your organization'. Bennis and Nanus (1985: 89) argue:

Note also that a vision always refers to a future state, a condition that does not presently exist and never existed before. With a vision, the leader provides the all-important bridge from the present to the future.

This is supported by writers such as Westley and Mintzberg (1990: 9) who see vision as a 'desired future organizational state'. Ironically, John Major, leader of the Conservative government's re-election campaign in the 1990s, had the vision statement of 'back to basics', probably one of the few vision statements that looked back! Put simply, vision is where you want to be in the future, what your school will look like, how it will feel to be there, what aspirations it will have and by what values it will operate. Nanus (1992: 16–18) articulates the advantage of having a vision for the organization:

- The right vision attracts commitment and energizes people.
- The right vision creates meaning in peoples' lives.
- The right vision establishes a standard of excellence.
- The right vision bridges the present and the future.

Gratton (2000: 13) uses powerful images to set the past, present and future in context:

> *in the memories and commitments of the past, in the excitement of the present, and in the dreams and hopes of the future ... Our memory of the past is balanced by a 'memory of the future', captured in our daydreams and the vignettes we paint to think through our options and the way we would like to see our life develop.*

Bolman and Deal (1995: 12) in their inspirational book *Leading with Soul* emphasize the emotional side of leadership:

> *Heart, hope and faith, rooted in soul and spirit, are necessary for today's managers to become tomorrows' leaders, for today's sterile bureaucracies to become tomorrow's communities of meaning ...*

This idea highlights one of the key elements of a vision, in that it creates a sense of meaning and pupose for individuals within the school and something to which they can commit. Leaders in the NCSL research study, when talking about their concept of vision said:

> *I've always had this kind of vision – a kind of concept of what can we do, what can we achieve as possible and then making it a reality.*

> *I have a sense of purpose in terms of where the school needs to go to be successful in the future.*

My vision was that I wanted a vibrant staff, a sharing staff; I wanted a different learning environment for the children, something that would incorporate different learning styles. I wanted parental and community involvement and I really wanted people to work – really work and not just be there to collect their salary, because there had been a culture of that, and those things are all starting to happen.

In a powerful articulation of the difference between leadership and management, Bennis and Nanus (1985: 92–3) argue that the creation of a vision and a sense of meaning is one of the distinguishing features of leadership:

By focusing attention on a vision, the leader operates on the emotional and spiritual resources of the organization, on its values, commitment, and aspirations ... leaders often inspire their followers to high levels of achievement by showing them how their work contributes to worthwhile ends. It is an emotional appeal to some of the most fundamental of human needs – the need to be important, to make a difference, to feel useful, to be part of a successful and worthwhile enterprise.

Brubaker (2005: 6) supports this perspective considering that the leader who articulates a credible vision 'creates conditions under which others feel inspired and committed to something greater than themselves'. He goes on to articulate the need for leaders to 'communicate their visions in a way that their followers feel new energy and a shared responsibility and a shared accountability'.

Lansberg (2000: 11) sees the leadership of organizations working through a process of vision on to action shown in Figure 3.1. He sees vision as a process of creating meaning through imagery, seeding ideas and testing them. Inspiration involves engaging individuals and building trust, while momentum is encouraging initiative, galvanizing progress and clearing the way for change.

Figure 3.1 *Vision into action*

Campbell and Yeung (1990) articulate a powerful model of linking vision and values in their account of the Ashridge vision and values model, shown in Figure 3.2. The purpose element in Figure 3.2 represents why the organization exists, what its vision is and what it is trying to do. The values are in what the organization believes. The standards are the policies and the behaviour patterns which govern how the organization operates. The strategy is the means of achieving the organization's purpose. This is a useful model for linking vision into action.

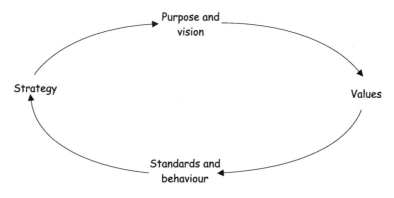

Figure 3.2 *Ashridge vision and values model*

Baum et al. (1998) report that what makes a difference to organizational performance is a vision which is brief, clear and desirable, contains relevant imagery, and is communicated and implemented by personal commitment. According to Baum et al. (1998), vision is far more powerful than charisma or personality in its effects in the performance and attitudes of followers. Gill (2001: 2–4) sees the importance of linking vision to strategy:

Without strategies, vision is a dream. Strategies are ways of pursuing the vision, identifying and exploiting opportunities, and responding to threats … Strategic plans, however, are merely road maps which rapidly become obsolete. Of more importance in strategic planning than road maps is the compass, which provides direction in line with our vision.

Gill (2001: 2–4) also supports the idea that vision is both rational and emotional:

Creating a vision is an intellectual and entrepreneurial exercise, which requires validity in the minds and hearts of followers for the vision to be an effective driving force. And for it to work, vision has to be translated into action and results. This is done through strategies and communications. Effective leaders communicate a rational appealing vision of the future and show the way through strategies. They 'do the right thing'.

The overall vision for the school should be a unifying concept, but to make it an ethical or moral vision it needs to be based on a set of values and beliefs. In the next part of the chapter we consider values and beliefs.

Values and beliefs

One of the most inspiring and gifted educationalists that I have worked with is Terry Deal, and his book with Kent Peterson (1999: 26), *Shaping School Culture*, provides excellent definitions of values and beliefs:

Values *are the conscious expressions of what an organization stands for. Values define a standard of goodness, quality or excellence that undergirds behavior and decision making, and what people care about. Values are not simply goals or outcomes; values are a deeper sense of what is important. Without an existing commitment, everything is relative; values focus attention and define success.*

Beliefs *are how we comprehend and deal with the world around us. They are 'consciously held, cognitive views about truth and reality' (Ott, 1989: 39). Beliefs originate in group and personal experiences and through reading books and articles. Beliefs are powerful in schools because they represent the core understandings about student capacity (immutable or alterable), teacher responsibility for learning (little or lot), expert sources of teacher knowledge (experience, research, or intuition), and educational success (will never happen or is achievable).*

The importance of core values was highlighted by leaders in the NCSL study, with a number of perceptive comments:

Never, ever to lose sight of the number one objective – education of children.

Identifying our moral purpose and then working out from that.

You also need to know you need to look at yourself and find out what your core values are because if you try and work outside your own value system it's not going to work. And you shouldn't take on a headship if the governors don't know what are your non-negotiables in terms of values.

If the concept is, and it is in this school, that at any time, any member of the school may be called upon to lead the school, and in fact we are all doing it – because if you go into any classroom, anybody who is actually leading – therefore in order to ensure consistency and direction then it has to be within certain agreed values.

The ethos of the school is not about merely giving our children an edge over everybody else. It's all actually about servant leadership – it's about encouraging these children to have a vision to use their talents, which undoubtedly they have, to serve the communities they may be in and not to use it as an entirely selfish way forward.

These are powerful comments by school leaders for both the importance and relevance of values as a starting point for all strategic decisions.

Beliefs are statements or views that help us set our personal views and experiences into context. For example, in conversations with John Novak (2002) he articulated to me three of his basic beliefs:

- People are able, valuable and responsible and should be treated accordingly.
- Educating should be a collaborative and co-operative activity.
- The process is the product in the making.

My beliefs regarding education of children would be founded on that:

- I believe every child can achieve.
- I believe every child will achieve.

- I believe that all children are entitled to high-quality education and a balanced curriculum.
- I believe that we collectively and individually can make a difference to children's learning.

A school example

Values need to be articulated and shared. One school I work with used a training day with staff to build a values grid. This involves a series of discussions to put into the grid the key words that sum up their values. This grid is then used with students and parents as a basis for addition and deletions before a set of value statements can be written down. The contribution of this discussion to creating common understanding of shared values is immense. The initial grid from the school is shown in Figure 3.3.

Respect	Honesty	Fairness	Diversity
Moral choices	Humility	Responsibility	Caring
Empathy	Compassion	Tolerance	Diligence
Independence	Perseverance	Interdependence	Trust
Kindness	Achievement	Challenge	Co-operation

Figure 3.3 *A values grid*

The importance of working through this sort of exercise is to answer the question of 'strategy for what?'. By that I mean strategy is not a function or an end in itself but must serve the core values of the organization. This exercise is a very powerful way for individuals in the school to articulate the values that they hold central to the pupose of the school, together with the values to which they aspire and wish to foster. This is a good place for schools to start from when they come to reaffirm and redefine their values.

What do belief statements in schools look like? Figure 3.4 provides an exemplar of a school belief statement.

School beliefs

Our central purpose is to provide quality learning experiences through a child-centred education. In order to achieve this we believe that:

- the needs of the children come first;
- everyone in our school community is special and important;
- each of us works to improve on our previous bests;
- learning is active, meaningful and creative;
- we have high expectations of ourselves and each other;
- we work well in a stimulating learning environment.

At our school we believe that every child will:

- be successful and confident;
- be self aware and co-operative;
- have a continuing love of learning;
- be independent and be able to work together;
- be a solution finder;
- be creative.

Figure 3.4 *A school belief statement*

Framing values and beliefs into an action is a key task of strategic leadership. Having considered an initial understanding of values and beliefs, it is important to look at some of the criteria that will help change broad concepts into practical applications. Freedman (2003: 52) makes some valuable comments about the applicability of values and beliefs. In applying what he calls 'basic beliefs' to action, he sets out six characteristics that facilitate the transfer from theory to action. I have adapted these to a school context. To be strategically useful, schools basic beliefs must be:

1. *Universal*. Basic beliefs apply to every level in the school, to every student and every employee, every function, and every location, with no exceptions.
2. *Realistic*. Although no organization is perfect, its basic beliefs should express attainable goals for continuous implementation.
3. *Clearly stated and easily understood*. If a basic belief is ambiguous or couched in jargon, it is meaningless. Everyone should be able to grasp the intent of each basic belief.
4. *Measurable*. A basic belief should identify distinctly the kinds of observable behaviours and standards that will be used to assess how all in the school behave and interact.
5. *Demonstrable*. Everyone should be able to see the basic beliefs 'in action'. Role modelling by leaders is especially crucial; without it they will rightly be accused of producing a package that is all pomp and no circumstance.
6. *Consequential*. Quite simply if a school's basic beliefs have no impact on its decision-making, they are irrelevant. Basic beliefs are a powerful strategic unifier only when they are owned and implemented through the school.

These six characteristics provide a useful checklist for a school when it comes to write its belief statement. They also make the process of translating beliefs into action easier. Statements in a school prospectus have meaning only if they are part of the lived experience of all those who work and learn in the school. Therefore, the clarity and reality of those beliefs need to be expressed in such a way as to make them operable in a meaningful way.

Values and beliefs and the leader

Building a set of values and beliefs in an organization will be successful only if the leader is perceived to be acting within a moral framework. Kouzes and Posner (1999: 49) argue that 'human beings don't put their hearts into something they don't believe in'. Their research into values puts forward the view that it is the clarity of an individual's values that makes a difference to their level of commitment to the organization. Where these coincide with the clarity of organizational values then there is the highest level of commitment. Interestingly, where there are high levels of clarity of personal values but some confusion over organizational values there is still high level of commitment, but where clarity of organizational values is not supported by high levels of personal values then commitment is limited. What values or moral characteristics do leaders need to establish the moral culture of the organization?

Brubaker and Colbe (2005: 176–81), in discussing the components of the moral culture, draw on research by Josephson (1991) to outline core values that respondents found desirable in ethical leaders. I outline each of them in turn:

- Honesty – that colleagues can rely on what you say is the truth.
- Integrity – words and actions are aligned.
- Promise keeping – the ability to deliver on what you agree to do.
- Loyalty – to the organization you work for and the people who you work with.
- Fairness – you have the same set of expectations from all staff.
- Concern for others – in their working and personal lives.
- Respect for others – respecting their individual differences and diversity.
- Law abiding – operating within the accountability and regulatory frameworks.
- Pursuit of excellence – striving for high achievements by all staff and students.
- Personal accountability – take responsibility, admit mistakes and share success.

In establishing a set of values and beliefs the leader not only has to demonstrate, establish and espouse the values themselves, but also has to communicate these to others. One way of looking at this is that these values and beliefs will be in the strategic documentation but, most significantly, they will be part of the school culture. Deal and Peterson (1999: 1) when looking at school culture see:

> *The culture of an enterprise plays the dominant role in extemporary performance. Highly respected organizations have evolved a shared system*

of informal folkways and traditions that infuse work with meaning, passion and purpose.

When school leaders come to enrich a school culture with values and beliefs for its strategic journey, Deal and Peterson (1999: 87) see that school leaders take on eight major symbolic roles:

1 Historian – understanding where the school has come from and why it behaves currently as it does.
2 Anthropological sleuth – seeks to understand the current set of norms, values and beliefs that define the current culture.
3 Visionary – works with others to define a deeply value-focused picture of the future for the school.
4 Symbol – affirms values through dress, behaviour, attention and routines.
5 Potter – shapes and is shaped by the school's heroes, rituals, traditions, ceremonies, symbols; brings in staff who share core values.
6 Poet – uses language to reinforce values and sustains the school's best image of itself.
7 Actor – improvises in the school's inevitable dramas, comedies and tragedies.
8 Healer – oversees transitions and changes in the life of the school; heals wounds of conflict and loss.

There is a danger that we see strategy as a boring planning process. Nothing could be further from the truth. Strategy needs passion and commitment and, above all, a desire to embed a set of moral purpose, values and beliefs into the educational process. Thus the role of the strategic leader is to embody the eight roles outlined by Deal and Peterson in order to translate not only the documentation and frameworks of strategy, but also the culture and meaning of the human experience. In doing so the leader works through and develops a set of school values and beliefs.

Setting values and beliefs in a strategic context

John MacBeath (2004) is a reflective and perceptive commentator on the educational field in the UK and overseas. In an insightful lecture at the Second International Summit for Leadership in Education in

Boston, he posed two frameworks for considering the nature of strategic change impacting on schools, and the management paradoxes in which leaders had to lead. In both of these frameworks the nature of the change and the paradoxes faced are underpinned by how leaders respond based on their values and beliefs. We will consider each in turn.

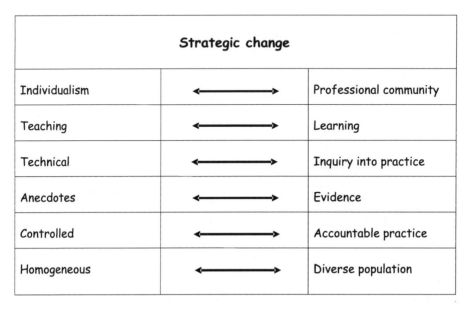

Figure 3.5 *Strategic change (MacBeath, 2004)*

In the framework on strategic change, shown in Figure 3.5, MacBeath sees a trend or move from one type of practice or emphasis to another. The traditional role of the teacher with autonomy and professional independence is moving towards a more integrated professional community. Emphasis on the teaching role is being replaced by emphasis on the learning approach. How do changes like this affect the teachers in the school? How do they reconceptualize their belief in their role and how it is changing? Are their values based on a self-image of the expert dispensing knowledge or a learning guide? Similarly, do they value technical skills or do they believe in constant enquiry into practice to reframe their understanding? Do leaders believe they need to control the actions of staff or do they operate systems of professional accountability? Are the values that the school holds about the children they teach challenged when a homogeneous group of students is replaced over time with a more diverse population with different cultural and belief systems? How do schools reassess their values and beliefs in these contexts? We saw earlier that values can be seen as 'conscious expressions of what an organization stands for' and beliefs as 'how we comprehend and deal with the world around us'. This emphasizes that schools need to consider strategic change in terms of its functional impact and how such changes impact on the values and beliefs of the school.

The value and belief system of the school leader is brought into sharp focus when the challenge of leading and managing in a paradoxical environment is considered. MacBeath puts forward this framework to highlight the nature of the paradox in Figure 3.6.

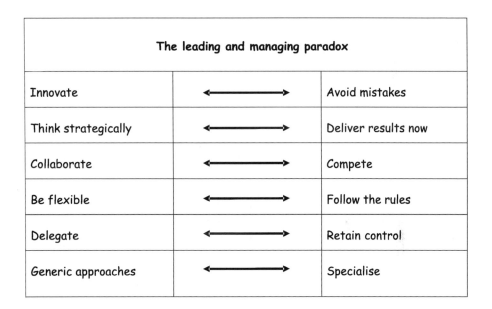

The leading and managing paradox		
Innovate	←——————→	Avoid mistakes
Think strategically	←——————→	Deliver results now
Collaborate	←——————→	Compete
Be flexible	←——————→	Follow the rules
Delegate	←——————→	Retain control
Generic approaches	←——————→	Specialise

Figure 3.6 *The leadership and management paradox (MacBeath, 2004)*

These paradox situations provide significant leadership challenges. Leaders face short-term pressures to deliver SATs and other examination results that could be achieved with replication of shallow learning. However, their value system may be based on a value of deep understanding of learning and nurturing a love of learning in their children. This latter may be a longer-term strategic objective which they work towards, but how do they address the short-term pressures without conflicting with their values and beliefs? The value-based approach of believing that a school has a responsibility not only for the education of its own children but is also part of a local and regional education system and has wider responsibilities is often brought into conflict if it finds itself in a competitive market environment for students. The ethical stance it takes, based on its value system, will be a critical backcloth for its short-term decisions. Issues of the degree of flexibility and the amount of responsibility leader's wish to delegate to colleagues may conflict with external requirements. Finally, the move in the secondary sector in the UK from a generic approach to a broad curriculum experience is being replaced by every school being encouraged to be a specialist school. How does this affect an individual school's view of the value of education?

Conclusion

The lesson of these two frameworks of strategic change and the leading and managing paradox is that values and beliefs underpin all that we do. While strategy provides the framework and the means to move the school forward, movement or change must be based on a clear value and belief system. Schools are about providing education for the whole child in a moral and sustainable environment. Defining the values and beliefs of the school is a prerequisite of the strategic process. It is necessary to answer the question of 'strategy for what?' before we attempt to look at the 'how' of strategy.

In the Peter and Jane case study, in Chapter 2, it can be seen that Jane practises values-based leadership, and it is a cornerstone of all that she does. This is not always the case with Peter, where short-termism and pragmatic responses undermine the value base of many of his actions. So the implication for Jane is that her values and beliefs are an invaluable compass in turbulent leadership times.

Strategic processes: overview

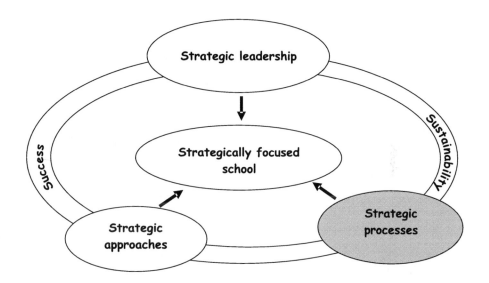

Overview of all the strategic processes

When we start on the journey of building a strategically focused school, a common initial mistake is to equate strategy with outcomes in terms of written plans. While such written plans and outcomes is an element of strategy, it is more critical to the success of any strategy that very significant attention is paid to the processes involved in developing that strategy. This is one of the key tasks of strategic leadership. How can we develop a strategic and sustainable framework for the future of the school? If this framework is to move into reality then it must both involve and inspire all those who work in the school. Questions such as: 'Who is involved in the strategic process?', 'How are they involved?' and 'How can the process be continuously evolving and developing and not be a static annual process undertaken once a year?' are critical for strategic success.

41

Gratton (2000) considers a three-stage model of strategy: first, where it is a top-down rational model coming from senior leaders; second, where it is a bottom- up model with strategy emerging from within the staff; and third, with strategy as a learning process that is structured to draw the best ideas from across the school. She recognizes the limitations of the top-down approach but is concerned about leaving strategy to emerge by chance from within the organization in the second stage. She advocates a middle ground suggesting that 'while it is not possible for managers to work out optimal strategies through rational thinking processes alone, they can create processes within organizations which guide the emergence of strategy' (Gratton, 2000: 47). This is a combination of setting frameworks but allowing flexibility to enable those frameworks to adapt and change with reality.

This book looks at approaches to strategy in Chapter 8 but whichever approach is used it is critical that the people in the organization share the values and believe in its purpose and are integrated into the strategic processes. What is significant for an effective strategic approach is to give very significant attention to the strategic processes involved. Gratton (2000: 47) makes a powerful statement:

> *The foundation of these processes is an individual's reflection on events and strategic conversations, their cognitive maps and sense making, and … they engage in active learning.*

All strategies must be 'led out' and communicated, but the central strategic leadership responsibility is that of establishing a set of strategic processes that will involve all those who work in the school to achieve a desirable and sustainable future for the school. What would these processes look like? Drawing on the NCSL research, three broad areas of processes emerged from the school case studies. First was how staff in schools think and make sense of the strategic situation and context of the school. This might be considered to be how staff conceptualize their strategic situation. Second was how they engage others in the school to build and implement a strategic framework. Third was how that strategy is articulated and communicated. This can be seen in Figure 4.1.

Each of the elements of strategic processes are considered in the following chapters as follows:

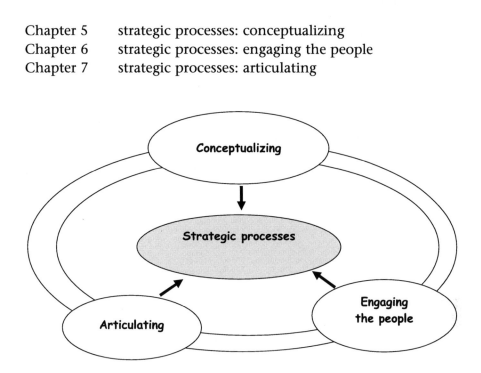

Figure 4.1 *Elements of strategic processes*

Chapter 5

Strategic processes: conceptualizing

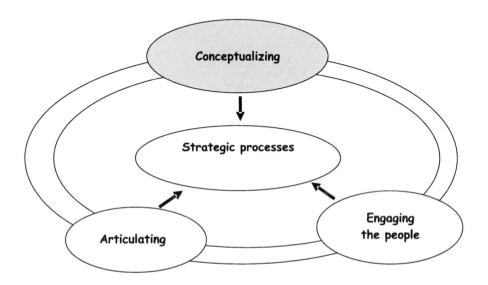

Introduction

What is involved in this first categorization of strategic processes: that of conceptualizing? The research suggests that individuals need first to make time for *reflection*. Leaders need to make time for themselves and others to stand back and consider how they as individuals and the school as a whole understand where they are. Individually, this would mean reflecting on their own skills and abilities and their ability to understand the dimensions of strategic leadership. This process then moves on to reflecting the organizational and educational context of the school and where it fits into the current environment. Building on this, the chapter then considers where the individuals and the school needs to be in the future, and this involves moving from the now of 'where we are' to the future of 'where we want to be' by engaging in individual and corporate *strategic thinking*. This strategic thinking involves breaking out of current mind-sets and making the conceptual leap to imaginative new possibilities and directions. Having started on the processes of strategic thinking, leaders will draw on *strategic analysis* to test their ideas, and attempt to build new understandings of their reality to form *new mental models* to clarify their new understanding. Figure 5.1 illustrates these elements but they should not be seen in a linear or sequential way. While showing the four elements separately in practice, they should be seen as interrelating and impacting on each other and on the central core of reconceptualizing the school process.

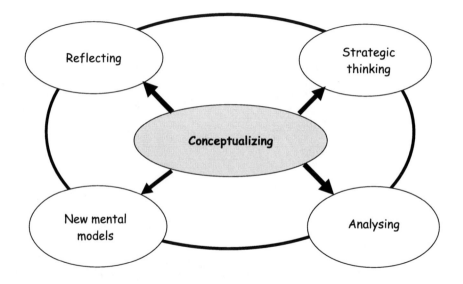

Figure 5.1 *The four dimensions of conceptualizing*

Having established the framework for the first of the process now let us look at each element in more detail. Figure 5.2 helps frame the discussion on each element.

The challenge for strategic leaders is to resist the temptation to rush in and start writing plans, but to stand back and do the important task of reflecting on the four conceptual questions listed in Figure 5.2. The analogy might be, the more time you spend on the preparations the easier the decorating will be! This first element of reflecting is now being considered.

Conceptual stages	Conceptual questions
Reflecting	Where are we?
Strategic thinking	Where could we be?
Strategic analysis	What do we know?
Mental models	How can we explain it?

Figure 5.2 *Conceptual stages and conceptual questions*

Reflecting: where are we?

How leaders in schools understand themselves and their school is a complex issue. Trying to understand their own self-perception and the impact they have on the school, together with where the school is in its culture and its development, let alone where it should be going, is a very challenging task. Stephen Covey's maxim 'Seek first to Understand, then to be Understood' (Covey, 1989: 235) is a pointed reminder of the need to reflect on our leadership and our school. Hamel and Prahalad (1994) when writing about the business sector could have been writing for school leadership. They state:

> So the urgent drives out the important; the future goes largely unexplored; and the capacity to act, rather than the capacity to think and imagine becomes the sole measure for leadership. (Hamel and Prahalad, 1994: 4–5)

This highlights the challenge of striving to be a strategic leader in a complex and increasingly demanding educational world. Increasing accountability demands and policy initiatives from central government mean that leaders very often tend to be reactive rather than proactive. This is especially true when the day-to-day challenge of staff and student issues impact on the strategic leader. However, the importance of attempting to 'ring-fence' time to allow the individual leader to understand what is happing to him/herself, the school and the wider economy and society is critical if the school is to move forward successfully. Novak (2002), in his perceptive account of invitational leadership, talks about 'inviting oneself personally and professionally' as a means of building personal capacity to both understand and cope with the demands of leadership. This he sees as the prerequisite before inviting others to join the educational journey. Claxton (2002) talks, in his *Building Learning Power*, about the four Rs of learning and the importance of the reflectiveness part of the learning process. MacGilchrist (2004) and her colleagues talk about 'reflective intelligence' comprising four aspects: creating time for reflection, self-evaluation, deep learning and feedback for learning. This is a process of creating time, to stand back in order to evaluate our own situation and practice, to get beneath the superficial and surface understanding and into deeper understanding, and to explore the meaning of our current understanding and experience. Strategic leaders in the NCSL study articulated views on creating time and understanding at different levels in the school:

> *Thursday is my reflection time and my reading time – I have been a headteacher now for 12 years. The first two years I ran around like a headless chicken trying to do everything and then I realized I was actually no good to the staff or myself and I decided to give myself a timetable to think ... Thursday is my time just to think, to read and to reflect and that's what I do. To be realistic it doesn't happen every single Thursday because sometimes when you walk through that door you don't know what is going to hit you.*

This is a powerful commentary on leaders making time from the management domain, of doing things effectively and efficiently, to dealing with the complexity of understanding what is going on and reflecting on its significance and putting that in the context of where the school wants to go. The challenge of trying to build deep understanding so as to be able to take the school forward is illustrated in this comment:

> *It's also about understanding – understanding the institution and understanding yourself, understanding the other players as well in the organization so that you can actually take the whole thing forward.*

This links to one of the concepts in strategic thinking, that of looking where we are now as well as looking to the future. How do schools build in this reflection? School leaders that I have worked with have changed their organizational structures and meetings to encompass a more reflective approach. This could, for example, be that, for ten minutes at the start of every key stage meeting or department meeting, one of the middle leaders explains the most significant learning experience by students in their area of responsibility over the past few weeks. By taking it in turns staff can reflect on their own practice and share it with others. This practice starts to build a reflective dialogue. Another approach is to take a set of meetings and make every fifth or sixth meeting move away from the normal organizational items and use it to review a major policy issue in the school. This way leaders build in reflection of practice as part of the life of the school.

Strategic thinking: where could we be?

When discussing the nature and dimensions of strategic thinking it is possible to make use of the work of many well-known writers in the field. We saw earlier in Chapter 2 the definition by Garratt (2003: 2) who gives an excellent definition of strategic thinking. This chapter also linked to Mintzberg's (2003) definition of strategic thinking as considering thinking as seeing. Thus strategic thinkers are individuals who are involved in 'seeing ahead', but also significantly 'seeing behind'. He considers that you cannot see ahead unless you can see behind because 'any good vision of the future has to be rooted in an understanding of the past' (Mintzberg, 2003: 67). He uses two other concepts that are useful to consider – 'seeing beyond', which he distinguishes from 'seeing ahead'. While 'seeing ahead' he characterizes as foreseeing an expected future by building a framework out of previous events, he considers 'seeing beyond' as constructing the future itself by inventing a world that would not otherwise be. His final idea of 'seeing it through' is very significant. Strategic thinking should have a result and an outcome or event, it should lead somewhere. Michael Fullan (2004) dedicates his strategic leadership book to 'Doers with big minds', using the idea of thinking and getting things done. Strategic thinking is a process where we build understanding and meaning about where we are and where we are going.

For the purpose of this book we will draw on these ideas and define strategic thinking as involving understanding the current context of the school, including its history, and building an understanding of where the school could be in the future by the use of new and innovative practices and policies. This could be considered as part of the visioning process.

The challenge is articulated very clearly by Charles Handy:

We are all prisoners of our past. It is hard to think of things except in the way we have always thought of them. But that solves no problems and seldom changes anything. (Handy, 1990: 54)

When I first started teaching in South London in 1971, my first staff meeting was made memorable through a comment by a member of staff about a new initiative being proposed by the headteacher. He said: 'I've been in this school since 1959, we've tried that before. It didn't work then and it won't work now.' When I relate this to headteachers on the leadership courses I run today, they all think the spirit of that member of staff has been cloned into their staffrooms! How do we enable ourselves and our colleagues not only to rethink their current situation, but also to make the leap and think strategically about the future?

Gratton (2000) talks about the capabilities that we need to build in organizations. These she considers are:

- visionary capability – school leaders need to build rich and inclusive dialogues about the future;
- scanning capability – developing an understanding of what the future may bring by establishing a broad and shared understanding of educational and societal trends;
- systemic capability – to see the school as a complex organization and to see what it could become as a whole and not just focusing on part of its activities.

Obviously, some strategic thinking takes place with the individual but leaders can facilitate a wider discussion by providing opportunities and frameworks to do this. It can take place in formal and informal ways. The informal ways in which the leaders within the organization share insights and ideas about the future of the school in conversations with their colleagues are critical. It is also making these activities part of the cycle of activities where inputs are provided to groups such as governors, senior staff and broader staff forums that provide the opportunity to discuss ideas and 'think aloud'. This is more of the right brain approach of capability development rather than the left brain approach of managing current systems.

Gratton (2000: 127) reminds us of three important factors if this strategic thinking is to work effectively and make a difference:

1 Look back from the future.
2 Keep the process simple.
3 Focus on a few themes which will make a real difference.

These are significant factors in strategy. We should avoid the tyranny of multiple objectives that make longer and longer lists, and being dominated by the current situation. Keeping it focused and futures orientated means we can make a difference in some key areas. Freedman (2003: 25) considers that we need to develop strategic thinking ability in ourselves and others. To do this he suggests we need several things:

Conceptual strength. The ability to think incisively and systematically about abstract matters.
A holistic perspective. The ability to see the whole picture without being constrained or misled by its various parts.
Creativity. The ability to think out of the box, to come up with radically new ideas, and to move beyond existing constructs.
Expressiveness. The ability to translate abstract thinking about the organization into clear words and pictures that are understood by others.
Tolerance for ambiguity. The ability to analyse effectively even when the information available is incomplete or conflicting, or when there is great pressure to adopt a particular solution.
A sense of stewardship for the future. The willingness to consider options that may sacrifice short-term gain to protect the organization's resources over time.

To develop strategic thinking in schools how do we utilize the powerful points from Friedman and Gratton? Leaders in schools need to pose questions that move the debate from how we deal with the urgent day-to-day problems, to the strategic future of the school. This involves strategic conversations (see Chapter 6) and restructuring the patterns of meetings and groups within the school, to reflect both the immediate and the strategic medium-term issues.

The importance of doing this was highlighted by one leader in the NCSL study:

I don't create enough time to think where we are going because you just get swamped by all the other things. But the solution is building in a capacity to allow yourself to do that.

Analysis: what do we know?

Strategic thinking, while drawing on the initial reflection process, will also need to utilize information on which to build understandings of possible future directions. To obtain this information the leader in the school will have to undertake a strategic analysis. Thus, *analysis* becomes another element of this initial strategic process of conceptualization.

Strategic analysis is a process of identifying where the school is now, where it wants to be and how that journey can be led and managed. The danger of leading a school, in the context of the standards and accountability regime, is that we seek quick analysis and quick solutions. However, strategic analysis seeks to identify how to build capacity and capability, to move the school from its present position to its desired future state. Sometimes this is more straightforward than others. This book compares rational approaches such as strategic planning, with capability-building measures such as strategic intent in Chapter 8, on strategic approaches. Here we shall consider building an analytical process. The rational approach to this analysis would be to work through the following four elements of reflecting, strategic thinking, strategic analysis and building mental models in a linear way. In practice the situation in most schools is more complex and the process is more iterative with feedback from one stage to another happening all the time, and thus the process is changing and adapting all the time.

Leaders in the NCSL study commented on the importance of the analysis stage as follows:

As well as that we had to convince all the parents it was a good school, that things were going well and so we did a lot of questionnaires, we gave children questionnaires; we looked at what would make a differ- ence. We did on-the-spot analysis with the teachers – you name it we did it. We brought in consultants to do a kind of mini-Ofsted to find out who were the good teachers, who were the weak teachers and we built on the evidence. We worked on the evidence to try and turn the school round.

We are a learning school – we are always analysing what we are doing, so a lot of the strategy comes through those review processes.

It is important that the analysis is broadly based and strategic. A useful warning from the business world about getting bogged down in current detail and missing the bigger picture is provided in the following account by Crianer and Dearlove (1998):

The turning-point came in 1983 when General Electric CEO Jack Welch dismantled the company's 200-strong planning department. Welch found the planners so preoccupied with financial and operating details that they failed to realize that the company's strategic position was being eroded.

At the analysis stage, it is necessary initially to operate a broad systems level where such approaches as STEEP can be used and where scanning the environment in the following domains can take place:

- Social environment;
- Technological environment;
- Educational environment;
- Economic environment;
- Political environment.

Davies and Ellison (2003: 49–80) provided detailed guidance of how this scanning can be done at international, national and local level. The next stage of analysis is to move to a more focused school level where analysing the parents' and students' wants and needs now and in the future is undertaken. This is closely linked to the school's ability and capacity to provide an educational product and service, both now and in the future. Schools have to involve themselves in data collection, and Davies and Ellison (2003: 49–80) provide a detailed account of various approaches and techniques that are available, such as:

- interviews and focus groups;
- questionnaires and attitude surveys;
- monitoring, evaluation and inspection reports;
- secondary data available locally or from national statistics and research reports.

Once this macro and micro stage of analysis and data collection has been undertaken it is necessary to bring the data together and turn them into useful information. One of the most powerful tools I have used for doing this, and starting a discussion on where the school is and where it should be going, is the Boston Consulting Group (BCG) matrix, which not only provides a means of bringing the analysis together, but is a significant tool to enable strategic conversations to take place. (The BCG matrix is discussed in detail in 'engaging the people' in Chapter 6).

This highlights one of the significant parts of developing a strategically focused school, of linking together a number of elements to build strategic capacity and capability in the school.

New mental models: how can we explain it?

The final part of the process of conceptualization is building a new framework for understanding, which we can describe as being a new cognitive map or mental model for the strategic leader; how we see and understand what is around us – what has changed and why. What does it look like now and what does it mean? How do we explain it to other people? Or, more importantly, how do we enable them to build their own new understandings?

One useful way of understanding this is to use the concept of mental models. These can be considered to be frameworks or pictures that provide a way through which we can understand the current situation. As we rethink our future path, using strategic thinking and drawing on strategic analysis, we build new frameworks or models that we can use to frame our own understanding and to provide a means of explaining it to others. Two of the leaders in the NCSL study commented:

It is about picking things apart, by using a model to base that thinking on, but if you haven't got anything there as a structure you are going to go all over the place.

It's the capacity of having heard a lot of things to be able to put that into a picture so others can understand it.

You know as the pennies start to drop with people, a lot of people need the concrete. They can't create a vision without me showing them something first.

New realities challenge and threaten the old. Wilson (1997: 1) states 'organisational change has two principal aspects – change in mission and strategy and change in culture and behaviour'. This could be interpreted as: it is fundamentally impossible to change mission and strategy without changing culture and behaviour. Key to this is to frame new ways of understanding by creating new mental models that explain the new challenges and solutions the school is meeting and establishing.

To take a practical and central question: what is the school's mental model of learning? How do staff visualize when that learning takes place? Does motivation lead to success or is it a series of small successes that builds motivation? How can we start to create a framework for understanding and build a new model for understanding?

Davies (2003) puts forward the ABCD approach to building a new mental model in Figure 5.3. The Davies approach works through a process in which leaders in schools make sense of what needs to be done, and where the school needs to go, and what the new ways of understanding are that the school needs to adopt. For example, a school may decide to rethink its teaching and learning policy. It would articulate this as a strategic objective. Through the process of reflection and strategic analysis the school might decide to build a new mental model of its approach to teaching and learning using the Accelerated Learning approach of Alistair Smith (1996). It needs to build within staff the images and the experiences of working with this new approach, and what it means for staff to conceptualize learning. To do so the school will organize visits to other schools, talk to colleagues in the profession who have used this approach and develop the language and the metaphors to explain what it means. It will then move on to creating a wider staff understanding of this new approach to learning by encouraging both structured and unstructured means of dialogue and communication in the school. Finally, a new understanding and a new mental model of learning will have been established.

The point of moving through this process is to establish a common, clearly understood, mental model of what the school thinks its future will be, and how it can explain that future to all those in the school community.

Articulate	1	Current understanding and desired new understanding
Build	2	Images Metaphors Experiences of desired new understanding
Create	3	Dialogue and conversations Shared concepts to frame new understandings
Define	4	Formal plans and frame of reference for the school

Figure 5.3 *Building new mental models (adapted from Davies, 2003)*

Conclusion

This chapter has looked at the four stages within the conceptualization paradigm of first reflecting then developing strategic thinking to lead into strategic analysis and, finally, creating new ways of understanding by building new mental models. Having started to unpack strategic processes by looking at the four stages of conceptualization the book now moves on to a consideration of how schools can engage all the people in the school more fully in the strategic processes. This is the vital task of engaging the people.

Chapter 6

Strategic processes: engaging the people

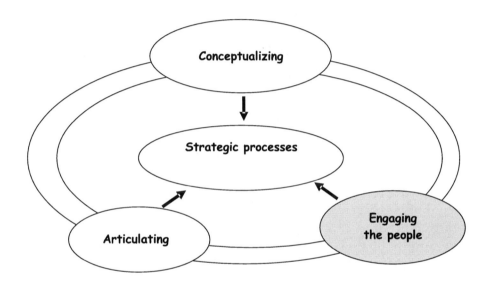

Introduction

When building and developing a strategically focused school, engaging the people within the school to be part of the process is vital for successful outcomes. Kouzes and Posner (1999: 29) make the powerful point: 'Leadership cannot be exercised from a distance. Leadership is a relationship, and relationships are formed only when people come into contact with each other.' How can we encourage individuals within the organization to engage with each other to build strategic understanding and enhance the strategic capability of the organization? This engagement can be seen to consist of four elements: strategic conversation, strategic participation, and strategic motivation leading to strategic capability.

The flow of participation

The most significant resource in any school are the people who work there. A key element in the design of a strategically focused school is how we engage the people in the thinking processes of undertaking current tasks and being part of a dialogue about what the school will look like in the future. One view of strategy is that it is not possible to predict all stages of development and outcomes. Another view is to let strategy emerge from individual behaviour, but this leaves a great deal to chance and is not very predictive. A middle way would suggest it is possible for leaders to both build an understanding of the major strategic development framework in the organization and at the same time create structures and processes which engage individuals within the school in dialogues and conversations about the strategic direction. This approach enables the school to be flexible and adaptive as it uses experience to adjust the direction and policy. Thus a process of fostering and developing strategic conversations, enhancing participation and motivation, will build enhanced strategic capability.

The most significant finding from the NCSL research and from reviews of the literature is the power of strategic conversations as a means of building strategic capability and capacity in schools. The relationship between conversations and their ability to enhance participation and motivation, as a means of increasing strategic capability, can be seen in Figure 6.1.

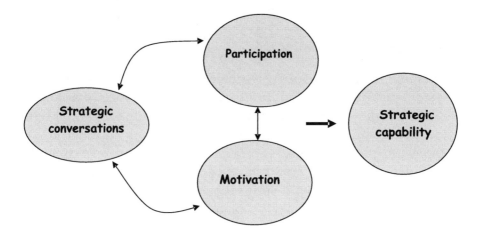

Figure 6.1 *Building strategic capability*

Strategic conversations

If we assume that schools are made up of different individuals who think about their role and the nature of the school in different ways, it may also be reasonable to assume that the school is not just a collection of these views but that, through the interaction of these individuals, a unique and powerful perspective can be developed to enhance the school.

Schools are a network of individuals linked together through a series of interconnections largely based on conversation. This is powerfully illustrated:

> *Often much more important is the informal learning activity consisting of unscheduled discussions, debate and conversation about strategic questions that goes on continuously at all levels in the organization. (Van Der Heijden, 1996: 273)*

What is required to create an effective individual and institutional conversation? The first way is for leaders to model behaviour. How do they interact with colleagues on a day-to-day basis? Do they just react to the current demands or do they engage people in thinking and talking about the future? Leaders need to take the informal opportunities to interact with others to discuss the problems of the present, but also to engage in a dialogue about the challenges of the future. The conversation over coffee or walking to the car park can be just as important as more formal meetings. It is also necessary to work with other leaders in the school to encourage them to do likewise so the culture in the school builds reflection and dialogue.

Leaders also have to make changes to the nature and pattern of meetings, so that the first item on the agenda is a strategic or future item and the meeting does not move too quickly into the day-to-day material. One good way is, in whole-staff meetings in primary schools or departmental meetings in secondary schools, for each person present to take it in turn to start the meeting spending ten minutes explaining their most significant example of student learning, to start a conversation on the nature of learning and where they need to go in the future. The danger is that the bigger strategic issue is tacked onto the end of a long agenda. My most vivid memory of a whole-school meeting was when we were asked to discuss two items. First, we were asked to consider whether boys should be allowed to play with large footballs in the upper playground. Second, we were asked to consider what the whole-school language policy was. By putting the football issue first we wasted valuable time and energy before moving on to the core strategic issue. How we structure meetings has a critical impact on the ability to engage in strategic conversations.

School leaders in the NCSL study made some powerful points:

With strategic conversations we have constructed a common vocabulary that helps to build a common vision. It is through that quite intensive personal contact with the key stakeholders to create an understanding that we could make things happen in the school.

So we have to keep having these conversations, but we have to have them at lots of different levels so that we keep everybody involved, carry everybody forward.

These two leadership voices highlight a number of significant points that emerge from developing strategic conversations:

- establishing a common vocabulary;
- understanding how staff could make things happen;
- consensus-building;
- outlining staff visions;
- building reflection;
- keeping everyone involved;
- carrying everyone forward.

How can we build an environment in which strategic conversations are sustained and developed? One of the most powerful tools I have used, working with school leaders, for building discussions and conversations is the Boston Consulting Group (BCG) matrix. While it is an analytical tool, the more I use it the more powerful I believe it is for stimulating strategic conversations.

The BCG matrix, used in a business context, has four dimensions: those items of outstanding success we call star products; those items that give us a reliable steady income we call cash cows; products that are not working out as well as we expected and of which we are unsure what to do next with we call problem children; products that are very unsuccessful we call dog products. The matrix can be seen in Figure 6.2.

Figure 6.2 *The BCG Matrix*

This matrix could be applied to schools as shown in Figure 6.3.

Outstanding elements in the school	Problematic areas: could be successful but not quite working out
Reliable or consistent elements in the school	Poor areas: Very unsuccessful

Figure 6.3 *BCG applied to schools*

The exercise involves asking participants to choose a series of items. These items could be products, processes or people. The products can be seen as what the school teaches, for example, the subjects or the skills. The relationships can be seen in a number of guises – for example, the relationships between governors and staff or between staff and students or among staff themselves. Finally, we could look at individual members of staff. Thinking about their own school, participants are asked to pick one of these categories (products, process or people) or a mixture of them. Then participants focus on the two most outstanding areas, then the two they would consider reliable, two where they have concerns and two where they were sure the school was performing badly. The first two stages are:

- to ask participants to put two items in each category for their school;
- to ask them to discuss their items with their fellow participants, with each participant sharing in turn their items in the four categories.

The discussion and debate is the crux of the exercise, and sufficient time should be allowed to build common understanding and create a coherent team view of the present state of the school.

The exercise then moves on with the participants considering what would have to be done to ensure that, if the exercise was repeated in four or five years' time, we sustain and reinforce the outstanding and reliable items, while addressing the problematic and poor areas. The point about strategy is that there is a need to build capability within the organization to undertake this process and to avoid the quick-fix solution.

In undertaking this exercise with governors, senior staff and middle leaders in schools, it can be seen that they immediately focus on the broader strategic needs and engage in conversations. It is the quality and the richness of the conversations that always impresses me the most. The next important finding is that it focuses a discussion on priorities. While we need to address areas for concern, it is important to remember the 80:20 rule. This suggests that 80 per cent of the organization is doing well and 20 per cent of the organization less well. However, we spend 80 per cent of our time addressing the 20 per cent of problems and ignore the 80 per cent that is doing well. As a result, this area of success can be neglected and can deteriorate.

This approach is, of course, taking the known and moving forward – as such it is only a starting point to get colleagues to talk about major focused items. It is then necessary to move to an exercise that enables colleagues in schools to 'look back from the future'. The looking back from the future activity can involve staff, parents, students or governors, or any combinations of these groups. The idea is to build a conversation and perspective of what the school will look like and what it should be doing when the students starting school this year will be in their final year at school. Use topics focusing on students' experiences such as:

- What will they learn?
- How will they learn?
- What sort of skills and abilities will they need to have?
- What sort of people do we want them to be?
- How will technology help them?
- What will the school buildings look like?

All these questions can be used to enable strategic conversations about the future of the school and to develop an approach that allows ideas to move to that desired future state. The final consideration would be to pose the question: 'If we were to repeat the BCG exercise in five years' time what differences would there be?'

Meetings, Bloody Meetings was the famous title of Video Arts management training programme on managing meetings. The theme of the training video is that people had meetings 'to meet' and that the meetings did not always serve a useful purpose. In schools we have both formal and informal meetings, and we need to make sure that meetings serve a strategic as well as an operational function. The informal meeting is just as important as the formal one as a vehicle for developing strategic conversations and ideas.

Strategic participation

There are two purposes for strategic conversations. The first is to draw in a wider group of individuals with their knowledge and expertise in order to increase the pool of ideas and insights that form the strategic discussion and debate. The second is to involve individuals in the strategic process so as to build involvement in and commitment to a desirable future direction for the school. These ideas are developed by Gratton (2000: 187) who articulates three powerful reasons for building strategic participation. These are using participation:

1 to build guiding coalitions. By this she means: 'The continued involvement of broad groups of people is crucial – to build management learning through involvement in the visioning process; to

map the causal relationships; and to become involved and committed to making the journey' (ibid.: 187).

2 to build the capacity to change. She sees this as 'being about creating genuine adaptation, developing an organization which is permanently adaptable and flexible and is involved at both the individual team and organizational levels, with a collective wish to move forward' (ibid.: 187).

3 to keep focusing on the strategic themes. This she interprets as 'The broad themes of the [strategic] journey act as a focus for action. This overview plays a crucial role in bridging from the present to the future. Perhaps most importantly it is a vehicle for communication, both across the teams and to the wide group that will be involved ... This overview ensures consistency of action across the organization ... ' (ibid.: 187).

Schools are dynamic interactive systems and individuals need to be both aware of the directions of the school and open-minded to change and development. They need to participate in varied and different levels of decision-making. Voices of leaders from the NCSL study talked persuasively about involving colleagues in a participatory framework:

I also wanted to see how far down the line I could really empower people in the school to be decision-makers.

They have to own it, get a feel for it and take it on. You have to consult because you've got to bring people with you. It's easier to lead than to push.

It's opened up a lot of discussion in team meetings which is good. I think it's because this year I have got a staff that are emotionally and personally attached to the school, where they haven't been previously.

Because of the high level of participation, because so much of it is ours, we feel much more in control of the agenda, I think that's where the strength of the school has come from.

Participation does not involve just teaching staff. Participation in developing the strategic direction of the school also involves a wider group as witnessed by the following from the NCSL study:

Strategy is something that needs to be discussed with everyone working in the school but not just the staff and I am a great believer in involving pupils because school is about children. For me everything that I do is about the children in my school which is about their learning.

Participation is seen as a 'good thing'. It does need, however, to be set in a broader organizational context. We could consider three levels of organizational involvement: those of information, consultation and information, as shown in Figure 6.4.

Level	Description
Information	Individuals in the school are kept abreast of major developments and the plans for future direction
Consultation	Individuals are told of the major directions of the school, consulted and involved in planning the details
Participation	Basic design questions are left open for full discussion and decision-making

Figure 6.4 *Levels of involvement*

It is neither feasible in terms of time available, nor desirable in every situation in terms of confidentiality, for staff and others to participate fully in every decision. In some areas information is the appropriate response, while in others consulting about different options or the details of design may be the best choice. If time and energy is to be devoted to the full participation route, then the participation should be genuine and relate to important issues that affect the long-term success of the school. As well as the nature of the involvement, the other factor which will affect the degree of participation may be the nature of the leaders themselves. Leaders may become more participative as they gain in experience. One of the leaders in the NCSL study commented:

> *My leadership style has become far more consensual as the school has moved on into a different phase. My first instance was, I suspect, fairly dogmatic, fairly structured, fairly linear in my handling of a very unpromising situation I inherited at the school, and then after the success that we have enjoyed and the camaraderie and collegiality that's been developed we were able to move on to a different phase, a different way of being, where we are more consensual and participative.*

Effective participation, therefore, may depend on the individual leader as well as on the situation. As such, a culture of participation and involvement needs to be built. Building the appropriate school culture is complex and a good analysis of this is provided by Terry Deal and Kent Peterson (1999) in their book *Shaping School Culture*.

Management was traditionally defined as 'getting things done through people'; strategic leadership in the 21st Century may better be conceptualized as getting things done with people. The 'with' involves building trust and a sense of purpose and involving all those who work in the school in the schools' strategic journey. The nature of the strategic participation both feeds into the level of strategic motivation and draws from that motivation to sustain itself. This will be considered next.

Strategic motivation

The purpose of strategic conversations is the greater involvement of individuals within the school to participate in the strategic development. This process will enhance the motivation of individuals to become involved in the strategic debate and implementation.

There are different ways we can think of strategy. At one level there are strategic frameworks and outlines. At another there are processes and approaches that lead to actions. Finally, there are the motivations and attitudes of the individuals who underpin the organization. This is often thought of as an iceberg where the biggest factor, motivations and attitudes, lie deepest and hidden, as shown in Figure 6.5.

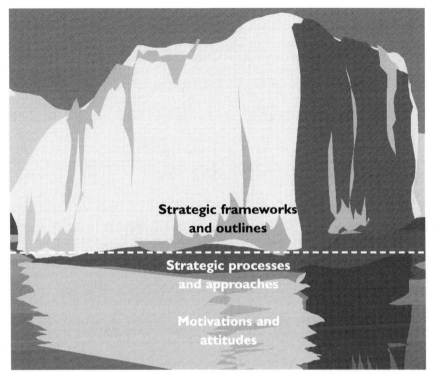

Figure 6.5 *Levels of policy and motivation*

The significance of involving and motivating staff was recognized by leaders in the NCSL study in the following observations:

People who are given the autonomy, given the freedom, given the responsibility, would actually add more to the value of the school.

What we have said is that this is all to do with improving learning and I think one thing is that a lot of people will probably say it's not workload it's because it's actually making them enjoy what they are already doing, giving them an understanding and control. One of the greatest causes of stress is not having the feeling you have control. What we are trying to do is to give people much more control over their destiny, over what they do.

I have some very motivated staff who are quite excited in respect of what we are really trying to do. To really think about what we are doing and where we are going and be part of that.

Empower people then they do astonishing things – way beyond expectations.

To a large extent the motivation of staff depends on factors such as:

* trust in the leadership of the school;
* sense of purpose – where we are going and why;
* feeling valued;
* feeling that their contribution is important and recognized;
* feeling that their contribution can make a difference.

These factors link very strongly with one of the characteristics of strategic leadership, which we shall look at in Chapter 9, that of the emotional intelligence of the leader. Developing these five factors is a critical part of establishing individual and group motivation.

The whole purpose of the three factors of conversation, participation and motivation is to enhance the strategic capacity of the school, which we look at next.

Strategic capability

It is useful to make a distinction between strategic capability and strategic capacity. Capacity may be thought of in terms of more teachers, more information and communication technology (ICT) equipment, new facilities, in general, increasing the amount of resources to build a strategically focused school. Strategic capability deals with enhanced levels of knowledge and understanding, which allow individuals to adapt to change and build new ways of working. While, obviously, we need more resources, those resources will have a minimal effect unless the abilities and attitudes of individuals can develop creative and meaningful solutions to enhance, and not just replicate, current practice. So, when we talk about strategic capability, it encompasses abilities such as:

* the ability to see the current situation of the school in a wider system context;
* the ability to recognize and utilize change;
* the ability to envisage an improved future scenario for the school;
* the ability to build effective relationships to create new understandings across the school;

▦ the ability to utilize resources in new and innovative ways.

There are other capabilities that could be discussed, but this provides an indicative list of the type of strategic capabilities that schools, which are strategically focused, will be trying to build. Leaders in the NCSL study reflected:

> *Leadership is about creating a culture within the school where everyone buys into the responsibility for where the school is now and where it is going.*

> *The more long-term things are those where you know where you want to get to, but you are not quite sure yet how you are going to do it, so you need to build some kind of capability within people. For instance, for 'learning how to learn' or 'developing a learning-focused school' requires a lot of people to change and to do that you need more time, so people need to go on courses, need to do some reading, need to build in some coaching and all that takes much longer. Once people learn how to do that, they have their own views about what a learning-focused school is, so then we have to come together and talk about it.*

Leaders in strategically focused schools are obviously working to improve the current situation in their schools. But, very significantly, they are developing strategic processes and approaches so as to enhance the capability of the school to move forward to new and improved learning opportunities for all children.

Conclusion

Engaging the people is a critical element in the strategic journey. Involving and motivating all in the school to work towards a sustainable and successful future is vital. Strategic frameworks and strategic thinking happens only if the people in the organization value them and want to contribute to their development. Strategic intents get built and strategic plans written only if the people in the organization are committed to them. However, the strategic future needs to be articulated and communicated, and that is discussed next.

Chapter 7

Strategic processes: articulating

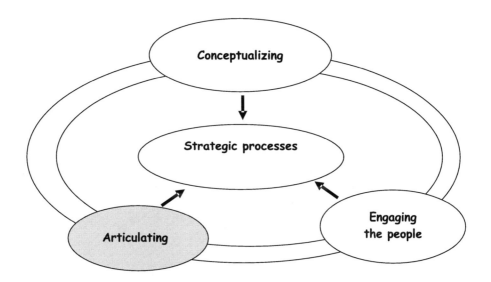

How we articulate and communicate the strategy for the school will be critical to its success. All those who are involved in the school should be able to understand the major direction in which the school is headed and should be able to articulate that strategy to the parental and wider community. There are three major ways in which this can take place: oral, written and structural, as shown in Figure 7.1.

Oral articulation

Oral communication very often is the most powerful means of communication. It is important that strategy becomes part of the language of the school. When this happens, strategy can be considered to have moved from theory into action. If a school has four or five major strategic goals or intents, and the staff are aware of these, they can clearly enter into discussions while building understanding and a sense of purpose for the school. The acid test for any strategy is to walk into a staffroom and ask staff what they think the major themes, directions or strategies the school is focusing on, and to receive a coherent answer. If you get 20 different answers you may consider it a diverse set of results. More likely it will suggest a lack of strategic focus and the lack of a common understanding of the major directions in which the school is headed.

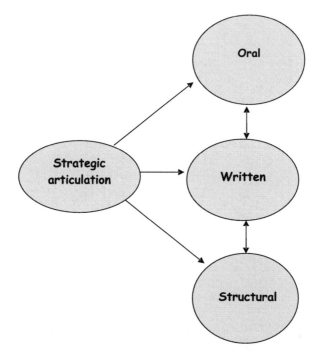

Figure 7.1 *The dimensions of articulation*

Headteachers often use formal meetings and workshops to articulate for staff the values of the school and its future direction and developments. Leaders in the NCSL study said they were using every opportunity both to build a common understanding of the strategy and, most importantly, to reinforce and refresh the collective memory of all those in the school community about the strategic direction of the school. Leaders said:

> *Every year at the beginning of each academic year I always go through the vision. On the training day I do an analysis of the vision – it's the college's vision.*

So the last year has been a process of bringing the senior management into the same framework of strategic thinking. Next September we have already got planned a programme of discussions and training sessions for the wider staff group.

As well as these formal opportunities, leaders also use informal conversations to establish ideas and explain current perspectives on key issues about what the school needs to do and how the school is going to do it. For example, leaders in the NCSL study commented:

I can, from my walks around the school, in my strategic discussions with people reinforce key ideas and discuss our strategy in an informal way.

Documentation is not as important as what people believe in and what people do, and for that you need constant conversations.

The formal communication though working parties and meetings are very important, but the significance of the informal day-to-day communication should never be underestimated. This can take place in a number of ways. Leaders of schools, in their attempt to refocus the culture of the school, use a series of leadership mantras. These are simple expressions of the core principals which the leader is trying to establish.

One leader I have worked with, on taking over a school with considerable problems, wanted to reculture the children's behaviour (which was poor) and the staff's attitude to children from an economically deprived area. As well as formal structures such as 'circle time' to provide children with the opportunity to express their views and issues and a positive behaviour policy, she utilized two leadership mantras. In discussing behavioural issues with children, she used the often repeated mantra 'What choices did you have?' and with staff who raised issues she used 'What is in the best interests of the children?' Why these two questions? The first is all about children changing their behaviour patterns. Instead of allowing children to blame their activities on other children, a leadership mantra is 'What choices did you have and make?' So if the child is reported to have hit another child, the leaders' response is 'Either you could react and hit the other child or you could stand back and talk to an adult – the choice you make and the consequences are your responsibility'. How you achieve a strategic aim of changing the behaviour patterns in the school is to translate, into conversations that children in the school can understand, the idea that they are responsible for their own actions. Similarly with staff, working towards the strategic aim of moving the culture to one of putting the child first, the headteacher seeks the staff view on solutions by asking 'What do you think is in the best interest of the child?' This engages the member of staff in reflecting on values and beliefs and ways of moving the organization forward.

The key lesson is that it is through the oral expression of conversations and discussions that strategy comes to life and becomes a reality to those working in the school. This section links with the concepts outlined earlier in our consideration of strategic conversations in Chapter 6.

Written

What plans need to be written down? Bearing in mind the maxim from Davies and Ellison (2003) that 'the thicker the plan the less it effects practice', what is it that can give a focused framework? Davies and Ellison put forward a three-stage framework for schools in the model shown in Figure 7.2.

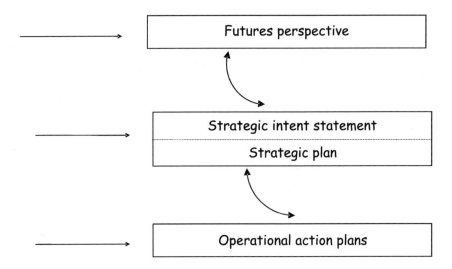

Figure 7.2 *The Davies and Ellison model*

This model suggests that schools operate at three levels. At the operational action plan level, schools have developed significant experience at what used to be called school development planning and is now more often referred to as school improvement planning. These short-term action plans are detailed and relate resource inputs to measurable learning outputs. The plans are usually framed in a one- to three-year time framework. In this book I am not addressing these short-term issues. This book suggests that schools should talk about a planning framework and that the written strategic framework is separate from the short-term operational plans. It suggests that two documents that might form the strategic framework are the strategic intent statement (see Chapter 8 Figures 8.6 and 8.7) and a strategic plan (Chapter 8 see Figures 8.1, 8.2 and 8.3). Finally, the Davies and Ellison model talks about a futures perspective. While the outlines of this can be written down, the critical part is a futures dialogue that builds the futures perspective and by its very nature it will be broad rather than detailed. The response a school leader should give to an Ofsted inspector who asks for a copy of the school development plan is: 'The school has a holistic planning framework and would she/he like to see the operation element or the strategic element of the framework or both?' Reminding ourselves of the characteristics of strategy, already established, that it should be direction setting, broad not detailed, a three-to five-year time frame and a template against which to set shorter-term actions, then the written strategic intents and strategic plans should be focused and concise as shown in Chapter 8. If these criteria can be met, it is then reasonable for staff to understand the broad parameters of the school's strategic framework, which is not possible if the detailed complexity of short-term planning is replicated.

School leaders in the research study commented;

The strategic plan for me was really something which the governors asked me to look at, and I resisted it for quite a while, and then began to see the value in something which wasn't the school development plan but actually was a much bigger picture of what the next 3–6 years might look like.

What we have found is that the better schools are doing this. They have a short-term plan and a separate corporate plan or strategic plan. These are separate documents.

CASE EXAMPLE: PRIMARY

An example of good practice in a primary school is shown in the following case.

The principles behind the structure are twofold: to allow time for focusing on the strategic and operational dimensions and to allow a wide range of staff and governors to engage in discussion, rather than limiting involvement to those in senior positions. This increases understanding but is also a powerful motivator for less experienced staff.

The school is driven by three strategic groups which form a strategic framework and planning process. The futures and strategy review group meets annually with governors (chair and sub-committee chairs) and the school leadership team (headteacher, deputy headteacher, Foundation Stage leader, KS1 leader, KS2 leader and SENCO). They review and set the long-term strategic direction of the school. The school leadership team meets termly to continue that review and direction setting process. The school also has team and task groups (research and improvement groups) to investigate new initiatives and projects that will inform future practice. These three groups feed into the overall strategic and operational framework of the school.

The operational part of the school's planning framework is seen in three further groups. The normal cycle of governors' meetings and sub-committees, the fortnightly leadership team meetings and the weekly staff meetings. This framework is designed to link strategic and operational planning so that the school can drive the short-term improvement in standards while developing the long-term capacity of the school.

Figure 7.3 *Primary case example of structural articulation (NCSL, 2005: 33)*

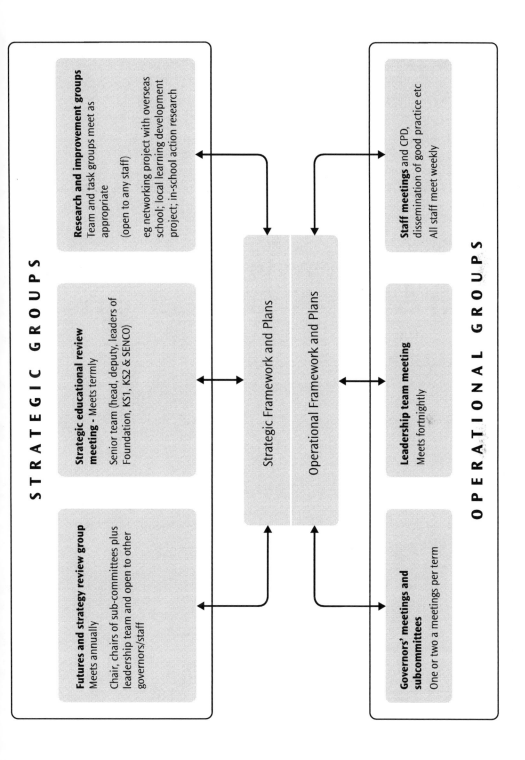

STRATEGIC GROUPS

Research and improvement groups
Team and task groups meet as appropriate

(open to any staff)

eg networking project with overseas school; local learning development project; in-school action research

Strategic educational review meeting - Meets termly

Senior team (head, deputy, leaders of Foundation, KS1, KS2 & SENCO)

Futures and strategy review group
Meets annually

Chair, chairs of sub-committees plus leadership team and open to other governors/staff

Strategic Framework and Plans

Operational Framework and Plans

Staff meetings and CPD, dissemination of good practice etc
All staff meet weekly

Leadership team meeting
Meets fortnightly

Governors' meetings and subcommittees
One or two a meetings per term

OPERATIONAL GROUPS

Figure 7.3 (*Continued*)

CASE EXAMPLE: SECONDARY

One school reported having an innovative management which emphasises quality assurance and continuous improvement and allows greater participation and involvement by all staff. Participation is not simply based on status or seniority but responsibility or the willingness to serve and be a creative thinker. The separation of the 'operational management team' from the 'strategic policy team' has proved to be a great success. Too often senior management teams become bogged down in operational matters with little or no time to discuss important strategic issues. The separation of strategic and operational functions has resulted in a separation of the urgent from the important. No longer does the urgent drive out the important; both are now catered for. In addition, the various teams provide a unique 'time horizon' management structure with:

■ 'operational management team' focusing on the next 0–12 months

■ 'school development plan team' focusing on the next six–24 months

■ 'research and development plan team' focusing on the next two–five years

Figure 7.4 *Secondary case example of structural articulation (NCSL, 2005: 32)*

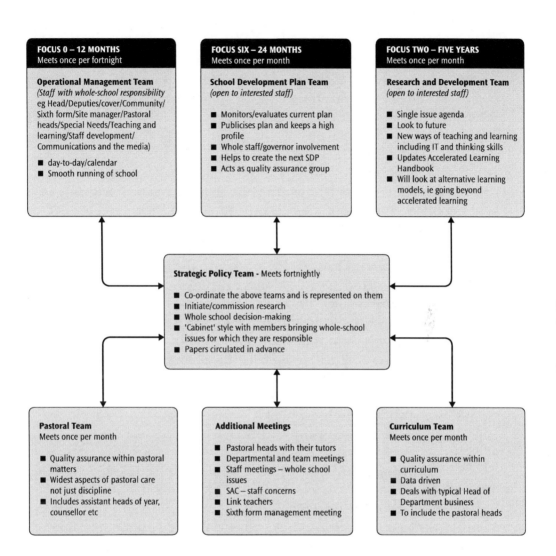

FOCUS 0 – 12 MONTHS
Meets once per fortnight

Operational Management Team
(Staff with whole-school responsibility eg Head/Deputies/cover/Community/Sixth form/Site manager/Pastoral heads/Special Needs/Teaching and learning/Staff development/Communications and the media)

- day-to-day/calendar
- Smooth running of school

FOCUS SIX – 24 MONTHS
Meets once per month

School Development Plan Team
(open to interested staff)

- Monitors/evaluates current plan
- Publicises plan and keeps a high profile
- Whole staff/governor involvement
- Helps to create the next SDP
- Acts as quality assurance group

FOCUS TWO – FIVE YEARS
Meets once per month

Research and Development Team
(open to interested staff)

- Single issue agenda
- Look to future
- New ways of teaching and learning including IT and thinking skills
- Updates Accelerated Learning Handbook
- Will look at alternative learning models, ie going beyond accelerated learning

Strategic Policy Team - Meets fortnightly

- Co-ordinate the above teams and is represented on them
- Initiate/commission research
- Whole school decision-making
- 'Cabinet' style with members bringing whole-school issues for which they are responsible
- Papers circulated in advance

Pastoral Team
Meets once per month

- Quality assurance within pastoral matters
- Widest aspects of pastoral care not just discipline
- Includes assistant heads of year, counsellor etc

Additional Meetings

- Pastoral heads with their tutors
- Departmental and team meetings
- Staff meetings – whole school issues
- SAC – staff concerns
- Link teachers
- Sixth form management meeting

Curriculum Team
Meets once per month

- Quality assurance within curriculum
- Data driven
- Deals with typical Head of Department business
- To include the pastoral heads

The 'school development plan team,' due to its composition, is more likely than any senior management team to know whether the development plan is working on the ground. It produces a continually updated picture of the school development plan in action. The R&D group has already proven to be invaluable, searching the world for world-class best practice and bringing it to the school. Its members regularly visit the United States for this purpose and £3,000 is put aside from the school budget to facilitate these visits. Currently the R&D team is doing action research in a number of different areas including home-learning projects as a substitute for the traditional homework tasks and different ways for teachers to assess students' work, for example audio assessment and training students in self-assessment techniques. The R&D team investigates researches and develops new ideas, the most successful of which are absorbed into our normal practice.

Figure 7.4 *(Continued)*

These leaders recognized the need to separate the operation and the strategic dimension of the overall school's planning framework. The leadership imperative is to have a limited number of strategic objectives and ensure that all staff are aware of them and that they are deliverable.

Structural

Articulating strategy through the structure that the school operates is a very important approach for leaders to emphasize the importance of strategy. It can be the simple measure of ensuring that in meetings on the longer-term strategy policy, issues are separated out from shorter-term operational ones. Alternatively, it can take the form of a more radical approach so different organizational structures encompass both the operational and the strategic dimensions of school life.

The two structures in Figures 7.3 and 7.4, from case study schools in the NCSL study, show how they have differentiated their strategic and operational structures. This structural articulation has two benefits: first, it allows staff to engage in the strategic debate and, secondly, by having the structures themselves, it demonstrates the importance and significance of strategy in the school.

Conclusion

It is vital that leaders in school do not consider that the articulation and communication of the strategic dimension is achieved when they publish their strategic framework document. Effective communication needs to ensure that the main concepts of the strategic priorities and direction are embedded in the organization. For this to be achieved there needs to be an ongoing dialogue of strategic conversations, to continue to reinforce and develop strategic understanding within the school. Most significantly, the way we structure interactions such as meetings and internal structures need to align the internal organization with the strategic needs of the school and close attention needs to be paid to organizational design if we are to build a strategically focused school.

Chapter 8

Strategic approaches

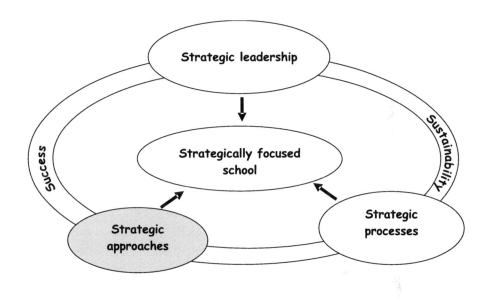

Introduction

This chapter considers three approaches to strategy which schools can use to move forward their strategic agenda. It is important to see the processes that are outlined in Chapters 4 to 7 set within a broad strategic approach. In this chapter we will consider how schools can use three strategic approaches. First, how they can rationally plan forward in a proactive and predictable way, using a strategic planning approach. Second, we will move on to how schools can learn from experience and develop strategy in a more reactive manner by using emergent strategy. Finally, we will look at a means of moving forward by setting strategic intents and building capability and capacity as a learning organization to deliver those intents. In summary therefore we will consider:

- strategic planning;
- emergent strategy;
- strategic intent.

It is important to realize at the outset that these are not alternative approaches in terms of undertaking one rather than another. Instead, schools may consider using one approach at a particular time and then another approach at a different time, or a school may use all three approaches concurrently. I have established a basic definition of strategy and considered the nature and dimensions of strategic thinking. We now consider the distinct characteristics of strategic planning, emergent strategy and strategic intent. We consider the main features of each approach initially and then look at an overall approach for a school

Strategic planning

Strategic planning is associated with a rational, direction-setting approach over the medium to long term. In particular it assumes that a school understands its strategic objectives (that is, it knows what it wants to do), it knows how to move towards those objectives (it knows the stages on the journey) and it has criteria to assess whether it has achieved those objectives (it has evaluation measures). Words that are associated with strategic planning are 'rational', 'linear' and 'predictable'.

It is important to distinguish between operational and strategic planning. School improvement planning is usually associated with a one- or two-year very detailed operational plan. To criticize school improvement plans for not being strategic is not a criticism, it is stating the obvious! We can consider a framework for conceptualizing this field as:

- Futures, 5–15 years;
- Strategy, 3–5 years;
- Operational, 1–3 years;

How would this look in a school? My research suggests that most schools have well-developed school development/improvement plans. These are very detailed and have specific targets, costs and evaluation criteria. They can be summed up as: who does what, when and how, and how we can check it has been completed. While extending this level of detail to a second year is possible, the ability to deliver the pre-specified detail by the third year of such plans becomes problematic. Operational planning is both desirable and necessary for schools effectively to deliver educational opportunities for their students. This detailed operational planning should not be confused with strategic planning. Strategic planning involves moving away from the detailed objectives to broader objectives. Futures is often the process of longer-term thinking about the nature of education and society that provides a backcloth against which to set strategic objectives. Strategic planning links the futures and the operational domains. While I have given approximate time frames for these three activities, it is important to regard them as just that: approximate. Considering them as frameworks for actions that blend into each other rather than having hard and sharp boundaries would be a useful perspective.

The first phase in developing a strategic plan for a school is to move away from the detailed lists and columns of the operational plan and stand back and consider what will be the major themes that will be driving the school forward over the medium term. This involves a fundamental review of the core priorities in the school and how they will be met in future years. It should not replicate the headings in the school development or improvement plan but involve rethinking longer-term objectives. In the NCSL research project our case study schools used five major strategic areas to structure their strategic plans. These areas are shown in Figure 8.1.

These lists act as indicative means of looking at how schools can categorize the way they define their strategic planning frameworks. If we return to our initial definition of strategy as providing a sense of direction in broad terms over the medium term, then strategic planning provides an integral part of that process. Some of a school's activities are predictable. Once students have entered the school they progress through the various age groups for the next five to seven years, and thus there is a degree of predictability on school roll. Similarly, annual refurbishment can be planned. It is highly likely that core subjects in the curriculum such as literacy and numeracy will also be the core subjects in five years' time. However, strategic plans do not usually concern themselves with activities where there is little understanding of the needs that have to be met. They tackle areas of development where schools have a good degree of understanding of what needs to be done and how it can be done. Strategic plans are a means of highlighting in broad terms these activities and articulating a means of achieving them. Case study plans from the NCSL study illustrate the nature of strategic plans with a primary school exemplar in Figure 8.2 and a secondary school exemplar in Figure 8.3.

Primary school	Secondary school
Children's attainment and learning	Standards and excellence
Staff support and development	Innovation
Pastoral support and home/community links	Community/customers
Leadership and governance	Income generation
School learning environment	Premises developments

Figure 8.1 *The main structure of a school strategic plan*

These plans highlight the nature of a strategic approach. They identify, at the outset, a limited number of strategic themes or areas to be developed. These areas are then broken down in order, more specifically to define the nature of the activity and the direction in which to proceed. As strategic plans are rational, predictable plans it is possible to define key outcomes and the expected time frame in which the outcomes will be delivered. Such plans also define the costs involved and it is necessary to nominate different individuals or groups to monitor and evaluate the progress being made. The primary and secondary plans differ in the major themes they are pursuing and this would be true of plans from individual schools. They are both similar, however, in the way the themes, or areas for development, are articulated in a coherent, defined and measurable way. However, while strategic planning is an important approach in strategy, it is not always possible to be able to plan ahead with full knowledge of what to do and how to do it. Also, the nature of rapid change in the educational environment means that schools have to react to externally imposed change. In such a situation a different approach may be more valuable and we look at that next.

Emergent strategy

Emergent strategy initially contains elements of a reactive approach. However, it can become a far more powerful approach when the school adopts the characteristics of a learning organization, becoming more reflective and, later, proactive in its stance. Emergent strategy assumes that schools often operate in an environment of change and turbulence, and have a number of initiatives or events thrust upon them. In such an environment schools do not always have the time fully to understand a new initiative before they have to introduce it. The learning process is done through learning by doing. It could be considered a trial-and-error process where the school tries new things, but occasionally there are errors. With a number of new activities undertaken by the school how can it learn by its experience? It has to set time aside to reflect on its actions; it can see that some actions were successful while others were less so. If a school can analyse experiences, it could determine which actions to repeat in the future (the successful ones) and which actions to abandon (the less successful ones). A pattern of successful behaviour emerges by building up a number of experiences and reflecting on them. By using that pattern of behaviour and actions, the strategy emerges through a reactive approach which starts to become proactive if schools learn from that experience and use it to set a framework for the future. This can be seen in Figure 8.4.

Over the last few years, initiatives such as performance related pay for teaching staff and the workforce remodelling agenda have been

MAJOR STRATEGY THEMES OR AREAS	NATURE OF DIRECTION/ACTIVITY	KEY OUTCOMES	TIME?	COST?	PERSON WITH OVERSIGHT
1. Children's attainment and learning	1a Raise standards of literacy	1a No child with reading age below chronological age, unless specific learning difficulty identified; x% at level 5 at the end of Year 6	3 years	These will depend on the scale of the individual school, the local context etc	This will be a senior member of staff as appropriate within the school's structure
	1b Involve all in extra-curricular activity	1b Strategy developed for full range of activities (creative, community, sporting etc).	3 years		
	1c Develop more flexible approaches to personalised learning	1c (i) SMT post established to lead this	1 year		
		(ii) Strategy for a more creative approach to learning activities developed and introduction commenced	2 years		
		(iii) Strategy fully implemented	4 years		
2. Staff support and development	2a Develop appropriate staffing capability and capacity for the school of the future	2a (i) Shadow structure designed for all posts	2 years		
		(ii) Structure implemented gradually	over 5 years		
	2b Ensure that all staff are competent in the latest ICT developments	2b Investment in leadership, technical support, hardware, professional development leading to significantly enhanced learning opportunities	3 years and ongoing		
3. Pastoral support and home/ community links	3a Develop opportunities for life-long learning for community members	3a (i) Community needs and appropriate funding identified	3-5 years		
		(ii) Space and facilities made available and activities established			
	3b Develop an extended school for children and families	3b Some links to 1b but also partnerships and space found for other activities/provision eg health and welfare	3 years		
4. Leadership and governance	4a Develop the leaders of the future	4a Programme of innovative development opportunities - internal and national - established for all staff	3 years		
	4b Senior team to be active in strategic networks	4b Active participation in national and international activities for all senior staff.	3 years		
	4c Increase the pool of availability for governor elections	4c Networks with community (parents, business etc) developed and interest encouraged in school	2-3 years		
5. School learning environment	5a Refurbish KS2 art/technology area	5a Designs completed, funds acquired and project implemented	2 years		
	5b New reception area	5b Designs completed, funds acquired and project implemented	4 years		

Figure 8.2 *Strategic plan exemplar – primary (NCSL, 2005: 47–8)*

MAJOR STRATEGY THEMES OR AREAS	NATURE OF DIRECTION/ACTIVITY	KEY OUTCOMES	TIME?	COST?	PERSON WITH OVERSIGHT
1. Standards and excellence	1a Key Stage 3 results	1a x% level 5 y% level 6 at the end of Year 9	3 years	These will depend on the scale of the individual school, the local context etc	This will be a senior member of staff as appropriate within the school's structure
	1b Key Stage 4 results	1b x% 5 GCSE A* to C; y% A* or A	5 years		
	1c Personalised learning	1c Personalised learning established for all	4 years		
	1d Administrative support	1d Dedicated administrative support in each subject area and Key Stage	3 years		
2. Innovation	2a Leading edge technology	2a ICT provision maintained and enhanced through internal support and external partnerships	Ongoing		
	2b Effective learning solutions	2b Most appropriate approaches to 1c created through linking knowledge from learning sciences, ICT, and staff	3 years		
	2c Reengineer staffing to meet new challenges	2c Staffing structure developed and adjusted in order to support 1c and 1d	3 years		
3. Community/customers	3a Support local community learning needs via learning opportunities, especially ICT	3a (i) Staff and space infrastructure established (ii) Opportunities identified, funding obtained and activities begun	2-4 years		
	3b All students involved in community projects – local or global	3b (i) Co-ordination procedures established (ii) Time provided to plan and implement	3 years		
4. Income generation	4a Increase student roll	4a Increased roll by 10%	5 years		
	4b Income generation	4b £100k generated per year from business to support ICT	5 years		
	4c Increase percentage of income from bidding	4c (i) Enhanced capacity for bid writing (ii) Income from non-core sources up 10% per year	3 years		
5. Premises developments	5a Joint community/school creative arts centre	5a (i) Proposal agreed	1 year		
		(ii) Plans finalised	2 years		
		(iii) Funds obtained	3 years		
		(iv) Building commencing	4 years		

Figure 8.3 *Strategic plan exemplar – secondary (NCSL, 2005: 49–50)*

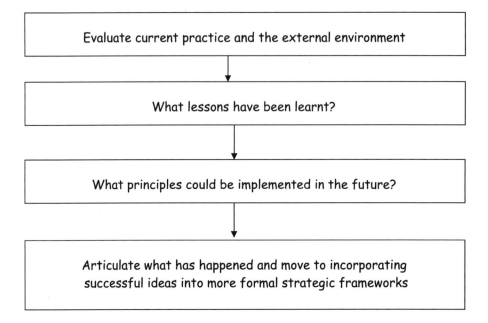

Figure 8.4 *Developing emergent strategy*

imposed on schools. While certain approaches can be gleaned from the legislation, and some more (and sometimes not!) from the training provided, much has to be learnt from experience. The two parts of these legislative initiatives that have to be understood are the implications of the individual changes and, most significantly, how these affect the overall staff management and developmental approach of the school. While part of this may be planned in advance, much has to be learnt from the experience of doing it. It is crucial that leaders make time to reflect on experience, draw out lessons that will form future patterns of actions, and begin to form strategic frameworks and directions from that information.

Mintzberg (1989) sees leaders less involved in *planning* strategy and more involved in *crafting* strategy. The key to a successful emergent approach is that leaders work to shape and create the future by constantly scanning the environment and analysing their own responses to it. Such an approach is needed because constant initiatives demand constant reappraisal and testing but, at the same time, leaders need to set these activities against a backdrop of futures thinking. As such, emergent strategy has a closer relationship to reality than an approach where strategy is reconsidered only at fixed time intervals. Leaders in the NCSL study reflected:

We are adapting as we go along and learning as we go along – emergent strategy is of course a learning process.

I think so many strategic plans fall down because they are too prescriptive and an event or a personal change happens and the whole thing is scuppered. You need to build strategy as you go along.

These insights from school leaders show the benefits of not being too prescriptive and the necessity of learning by doing. To incorporate the emergent approach into a school's repertoire of strategy, the leadership must set up regular and systematic reviews of the current situation with free and frank discussions of lessons learnt set against the direction where the school should be going in the future.

However, this approach can have its limitations. There are two concerns: first, it is leaving a great deal to the spontaneity of ideas and new frameworks emerging from leaders within the school; second, the incremental nature of change and improvement in strategy may miss the large 'strategic leap' that it is necessary for some schools to make. How can we integrate some of the proactive elements of strategic planning and the value of learning by doing of emergent strategy? Utilizing the concept of strategic intent is an excellent way of achieving this.

Strategic intent

Strategic intent is a powerful concept used to describe how a school can take a strategic perspective in a rapidly changing turbulent environment. It is a means of a school operating in a new and significantly different way. It can be considered as a means of 'leveraging up' performance. Just as a lever can create a significantly larger effect in moving an object, so intent can contribute to major shifts in an organization's performance. Strategic planning, as we have already considered, can be thought of as knowing where you want to go and knowing how to get there. Strategic intent would be knowing what major change we want but not yet knowing how to achieve it, but we will! It is a process of setting defined intents or objectives and committing the organization to a learning and development phase of how to achieve them. It is a framework for attacking difficult organizational change by energizing the organization into learning how to reach for new and challenging goals. Unlike vision and mission which are broad frameworks, strategic intents are more specific.

Strategic intents might be:

- creating an assessment for learning culture;
- reconceptualizing learning and teaching in the school;
- developing leadership in depth throughout the school;
- develop independent technology-based learning for all;
- creating and sustaining a high-achievement and success culture.

While initially these may seem straightforward, there needs to be a considerable discussion and analysis on the nature and dimensions of each of the categories and how to build capability to move towards achieving them. For example, setting *a strategic intent of creating an assessment* for *learning rather than an assessment* of *learning culture* is complex. Initially there is a need to establish what staff in the school collectively understands by the assessment for learning. The first stage would require the staff to understand where assessment fits into the following process:

Teaching input → Learning processes → Educational outcomes

Key Stage testing has resulted in many schools quite reasonably focusing on the educational-outcomes end of the process and, in particular, how these are measured in terms of pass rates. While this is an understandable and reasonable response, it has a negative side. By looking at assessment at the end of the process, we know how to change and improve things for the next cohort of students, but it obviously cannot assist the outcomes for the students who have come to the end of that particular learning cycle. However, if the school were to set up assessment processes and procedures as part of the learning process, students who were not progressing as well as expected could have their learning programme changed, and then outcomes could be affected. Moving to individualized learning plans and adjustments as part of the process is a far more powerful way of getting teachers to reconsider how best to approach each individual child. How staff achieve a new understanding to achieve this new strategic intent can be seen in Figure 8.5, where building and creating new understandings needs to come before the planning stage. It is this ability to set the intent and work towards a strategy rather than to seek a quick solution that defines strategic intent.

Before we look at another example we consider the four-stage strategic intent process in detail. Enabling staff in a school fundamentally to rethink their approach to assessment takes time and reflection. We saw earlier (Figure 5.3) the ABCD model with its four stages of Articulate – Build – Create – Define, and it is repeated in Figure 8.5.

Articulate	1	Current understanding and desired new strategy
Build	2	Images Metaphors Experiences of desired new understanding
Create	3	Dialogue and conversations Shared Understanding to frame new understandings
Define	4	Formal plans and frame of reference for the school

Figure 8.5 *Building strategic intents*

The key to building strategic intents is for leaders in the school to articulate the desired new objective (strategic intent) and to work through a process with staff of sharing experiences of good practice and developing images of what the new strategy can look like. By doing so the leaders will create a dialogue through strategic conversations to frame new understandings and where the school can be in the future. The school can then move to agreed formal plans on how to implement the new strategy. The whole process can take 18 months to two years fully to work out the appropriate strategy. The difference with strategic planning is that you go straight to level 4, but with strategic intent there is a major conceptual shift within the school on how to develop understanding and then significantly to improve and build the capacity to achieve change.

Another example of a strategic intent would be to *establish independent technology-based learning for all*. This may initially seem straightforward and may superficially elicit responses regarding the access to technology. A deeper analysis would reveal the importance of teachers perceiving themselves not just as deliverers of education, but also as guides to education. It would need all staff to have a positive attitude towards and competence in, technology. It would need the children to be active problem-solvers rather than passive attendees. It would involve the children having the confidence and skills necessary to be responsible for their own learning. The organization of the school day, the school and school year and the place of learning may also need to change. Once the articulation of the strategic intent has taken place, images of best practice need to be identified, conversations need to take place so the fundamental ramifications of this strategic change can take place. All these parameters need time to develop understanding and scenarios built before formal plans can be constructed.

In the NCSL study, we outlined how a school would identify the strategic intent of creating and sustaining a high-achievement and success culture. This strategic intent exemplar and framework is replicated in Figures 8.6 and 8.7.

Figure 8.6 shows a four-stage process. Initially intents are generated (SI: 1). These are intended to be significant strategic changes that move the school on in a fundamental way. Second, initial capabilities and capacity that need to be built are identified so that work can start to move the school towards achieving the intent (SI: 2). Stategic processes (SI: 3) are then engaged to build the intent. Finally, the school can move to implementation or identify more work to be done before that can be achieved.

Figure 8.7 outlines what needs to happen to deliver on the strategic intent of, for example, *creating a high achievement and success culture*. In SI: 1 the intent is outlined, and then the process of building and creating an understanding of the nature and dimensions of what the intent means and what needs to be done is seen to take place in SI: 2 and SI: 3

before implementation in SI: 4. This illustrates the key feature of strategic intent – that of knowing what you want to achieve but allowing time and introducing a process to build an understanding of what needs to be done.

Strategic intent, therefore, involves a major shift in the way a school operates. It necessitates a fundamental reappraisal of what we do and what are the key nature and dimensions of a change. It at first can seem obvious but, as staff unpack the deep meaning of the strategic change, then real and profound understanding needs to take place. Leaders in the NCSL research were powerful advocates of the strategic intent approach as witnessed by these comments:

> *What is really important about strategic intent is that it gives us an opportunity to say: 'Here are some areas that we are going to investigate.' These are perhaps some areas of development – it could be personal understanding, it could be about practice, it could be about wider reading, it could be about national initiatives. We don't quite know yet how that's going to pan out but in fact by identifying them now and saying let's give us a bit of thinking time, [we gain] some quality time to develop our thinking in these areas.*

> *I had to get them to stop thinking about 'but you can't go there because you need the route'. The intents are established first, and you don't know the pathway to get there initially. I actually think you don't make the big leaps if you know the steps you are going to get along the way. And I have a problem with target setting for that reason – right – that you always have to break down into little steps and you never think bigger than that.*

Strategic intent is a means of building capability and capacity for major change in the school. It is useful to utilize the concept of strategic capabilities and competencies to develop this analysis further.

Strategic intent and core competencies/strategic capabilities

The concept of core competencies in organizations is a very powerful one, articulated by Hamel and Prahalad (1994), and has parallels in the work of Stalk et al. (1992) who talk about strategic capability. The basic

In building strategic intents, the school will decide on a number of strategic intents that it wishes to establish and outline them at **SI 1**.

Each intent will then be taken separately to be developed (perhaps by different groups of staff or staff and other stakeholders).

The next stage is for intent to be developed as follows:

At **SI 2**, the school or sub-group will list the capabilities and capacities to be developed in order to achieve the intent. At the outset, some will be proposed while others will be identified at later points.

At **SI 3**, the school will note the initial process by which it is intended to build each capability or capacity. This involves proposing how it will be conceptualised (the thinking stage), how the individuals will be engaged in conversations and discussions around the possible actions (the discussion stage) and how any proposals will be articulated (the record stage). (This links in with the strategic processes on pages 15 to 33). It may be that, during these processes, there is recognition of the need to return to develop further capabilities or capacities as shown by the dashed line.

The possible next steps are suggested at **SI 4** of the framework. A decision will need to be taken as to whether the intent can be taken to phased implementation OR to full implementation OR other decisions could mean that the action is abandoned as inappropriate or requires further development. In the latter case, there is an arrow on the flowchart to take this back for further consideration at **SI 2**.

This links to the information on strategic processes on pp.34–41.

SI 1 GENERATE INTENTS

Generate a list of three to five strategic intents

These are intended to be significant changes and challenges that fundamentally move the school forwards.

1.
2.
3.
4.

SI 2 CAPABILITY/CAPACITY-BUILDING

For each intent (separately), list the early capabilities/capacities to be built in order to move towards achieving the intent.

1. capability/capacity to build now
2. capability/capacity to build now
3. capability/capacity to build now

4. leave for later identification
5. leave for later identification
6. leave for later identification
etc

SI 3 STRATEGIC PROCESSES TO BUILD INTENT

Take each capability/capacity to be built in SI 2 separately and set out the strategic processes which will be required to build it.

In each case this will involve the strategic processes (see pages 15 to 33) of

conceptualising; engaging; articulating

SI 4 IMPLEMENTATION

What is the next step?
Take decisions about implementation (or not) – how much progress has been made?

Is the school ready to:

■ move to phased implementation (see double S curve on page 37)

■ move to full implementation

■ abandon the ideas as non-feasible or no longer appropriate?

or does the school

■ require further development and capacity/capability building in this area

Figure 8.6 *Strategic intent framework (NCSL, 2005: 55–6)*

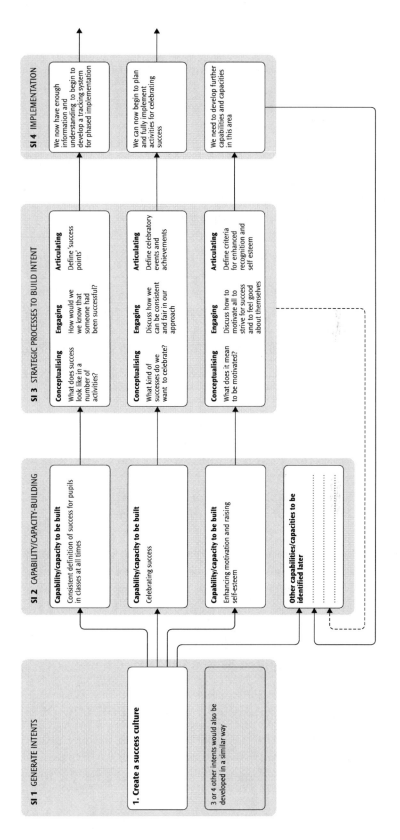

Figure 8.7 *Strategic intent exemplar (NCSL, 2005: 57–8)*

idea that underpins the concept of a core competency or strategic capability is that it is an underlying, deep-seated capability in the organization. The best analogy is that of a tree, where the trunk and branches are that part of the organization's products or skills that are immediately visible. They are supported by the roots which represent a set of abilities and attributes that underpin all that the organization does. Thus, in a school, the teachers may have an above-the-surface skill in teaching the latest version of the national numeracy or literacy strategy, but would need extra development if a new initiative was introduced. Examples of core competencies or strategic capabilities would be a fundamental understanding of teaching and learning or an ability to work as a team that would allow the school to tackle new developments from its own resources over a long period of time rather than waiting for short-term inputs from the external world. This can be seen in Figure 8.8.

The importance of strategic capabilities is shown in Figure 8.8. Here deep-seated strategic capabilities underpin the operation of the school in terms of its policies and approaches. Strategic capabilities such as

- a fundamental understanding of learning;
- high levels of trust and communication;
- using assessment for learning and not just assessment of learning,
- a creative and innovative culture;
- a positive team approach to problem-solving; and
- a learning and reflective school community

are core and profound attributes of successful and sustainable schools. These strategic capabilities are very complex and difficult to establish in schools. As such they depend on building long-term capacity for fundamental change and development. Using this strategic capabilities framework we can make a link to strategic intents in that they may provide the appropriate way of developing some of the organizational changes that are required in strategic capabilities.

A conceptual framework – integrating the perspectives

Useful theoretical work has been done in the field of strategy by Boisot (2003) who uses the three perspectives of strategy, as this chapter has, of strategic planning, emergent strategy and strategic intent. To these

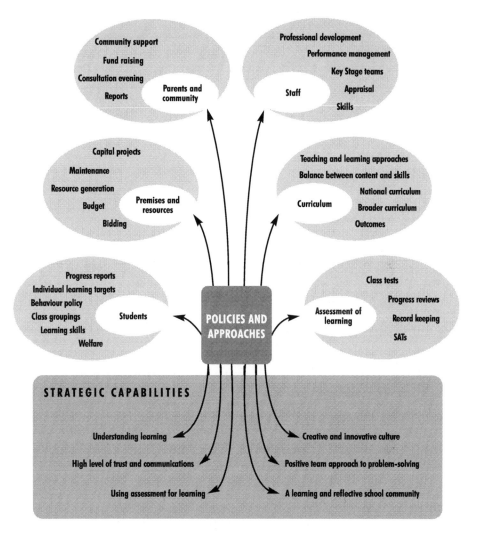

Figure 8.8 *Strategic capabilities underpinning the school's operation (NCSL, 2005)*

he adds a fourth perspective – that of decentralized strategy. With decentralized strategy those at the centre of the organization lay down a limited number of strategic values and aims and let the decentralized units deliver the strategic framework after that. I have not used this concept in this chapter as my research shows that it is little used in schools. In Figure 8.9 these four perspectives can be seen in the typology.

There are two axes in Figure 8.9. The vertical axis relates to the degree of educational and more general environmental change.

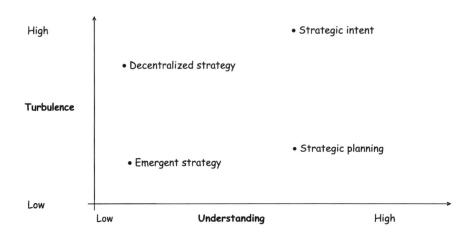

Figure 8.9 *Typology of strategies (adapted from Boisot, 2003: 40)*

Because change is often considered to be rational and linear, Boisot uses the term 'turbulence' to signify a more dynamic and unpredictable type of change. The horizontal axis relates to the level of understanding that an individual or an organization has of the turbulence and change in which it exists. Boisot articulates a model of strategy in which one of the four strategic responses or approaches is particularly appropriate to a specific combination of turbulence and understanding.

The critical feature of this conceptual model is that there is no right strategy. Different circumstances may mean that different strategies are appropriate. Where there is a high level of understanding and the level of change is medium to low, then a more predictable proactive approach can be used. When new educational initiatives are imposed on a school, little initial understanding will lead to an emergent strategy where schools learn by doing. Decentralized strategy may be appropriate in a very large organization where the centre has little understanding and therefore with high change has little option but to delegate major strategy development to sub-units. Finally, strategic intent can be used where there is a clear objective and knowledge of what needs to be achieved but high levels of change mean that capacity and capability need to be built to achieve those intents. Thus a combination of approaches can be the appropriate response depending on the situation at the time.

Conclusion

In the complex world of school leadership and management it is neither possible nor desirable to use one approach exclusively; what is needed is a portfolio of approaches. The demands of accountability frameworks mean that traditionally written plans are widely used. My research has, over the past 20 years, indicated that operational plans have become both more focused on learning outcomes but also more detailed and extensive. If we are to build a strategic framework for schools then we need first to acknowledge that detailed operational planning is part of the educational system. However, it would be a mistake to carry that level of detail over into strategic planning. This, by its very nature, should be a broad written plan for major areas of a school's development over the medium term. This can draw on the predictable areas of a school's development but also the learning from experience from the emergent strategy process. Most importantly, alongside this strategic plan should be a strategic intent statement which indicates major initiatives the school is developing and indicating how the work in progress is coming along. The danger for schools is the pressure to write down the predictable element and they will not give equal attention to the capacity and capability development work which is undertaken in the strategic intent framework.

In summary, my experience of working in and researching in schools which are strategically focused suggest they supplement their short-term school improvement plan with a strategic document that has a strategic planning and a strategic intent element. The key to effective strategic development is not the written document but the quality of the dialogue that goes to make up the strategic conversations in the school. Thus, linking the approaches to the process in strategy is vital. Reflecting on experience (emergent strategy) depends on the quality of conversations that take place just as the dialogue and reconceptualization that go to building strategic intents are also critical.

A school will need to formally plan some part of it strategic framework but it needs to outline the strategic intents it is working on to guide future development. As we saw earlier a useful comment for when the next Ofsted inspector calls might be:

Sorry we don't have a school development plan – that's reductionist twentieth-century thinking. What we do have is holistic planning processes with a strategic and operational focus. Which part do you wish to see first?

Chapter 9

Strategic leadership

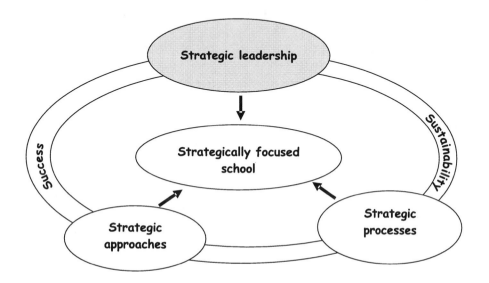

Introduction

The book has considered, in other chapters, strategic processes and strategic approaches; now we move on to the strategic leadership element. Strategic leadership is a critical component in the effective development of schools. This chapter builds on the ideas in Chapter 2 and puts forward the view that renewed attention should be paid to the strategic dimension of leadership, to ensure the long-term success of schools. The chapter addresses the issue of how the nature and dimensions of strategic leadership can be identified to provide a framework for developing a strategically focused school. The focus will be on the features of strategic leaders in terms of what they do and what characteristics they display. This chapter also highlights the leadership development implications of these activities and characteristics. Finally, the chapter articulates a new model of strategic leadership derived from Davies B.J. (2004).

Understanding strategy and strategic leadership

Chapter 2 considered that strategy involves taking a series of decisions which shape the direction of the organization. In a school setting we would see this as a medium- to longer-term activity, such as a three- to five-year view and beyond. Strategy also involves taking a perspective of broader core issues and themes for developments in the school, rather than the detail of day-to-day imperatives. Initially, it may be helpful to consider strategy as being aligned to strategic thinking and a strategic perspective, rather than just the traditional view of strategy being linked to mechanistic strategic plans. This perspective is taken in this chapter, seeing strategy and strategic planning as distinct concepts, putting forward the idea that strategy involves the development of a series of strategic *processes* that can ensure the effective development and deployment of strategy through the use of appropriate strategic *approaches*. These two elements are driven by effective strategic leadership in the organization. Schools that are successful in both the short and long term can be considered to be strategically focused, defined in this book as follows:

> *A strategically focused school is one that is educationally effective in the short term but has a clear framework and processes to translate core moral purpose and vision into excellent educational provision which is challenging and sustainable in the medium to long term. It has the leadership that enables short-term objectives to be met while concurrently building capability and capacity for the long term.*

Strategic leadership, by definition, links the strategic function with the leadership function. School leaders articulate the definition of the organization's moral purpose, which can be considered as 'why we do what we do'. The values that underpin this moral purpose are linked to the vision, considering 'where we want to be and what sort of organization we want to be in the future'. Strategic leadership is the means of linking this broad activity to shorter-term operational planning, thereby imbuing the responses to immediate events with elements of the value system and the longer-term strategic direction. Strategic leadership is, therefore, the ability to define the vision and moral purpose, and translate them into action. It is a means of building the direction and the capacity for the organization to achieve that directional shift or change. This translation requires a proactive transformational mind-set which strives for something better rather than the maintenance approach of transactional leadership.

These initial thoughts on leadership can suggest that it is strongly linked to the concept of vision. Beare et al. (1989: 99) argue that 'outstanding leaders have a vision of their schools – a mental picture of a preferred future – which is shared with all in the school community'. Four of their ten points about leadership focus on the vision dimension as follows:

- Outstanding leaders have a vision for their organizations.
- Vision must be communicated in a way which secures commitment among members of the organization.
- Communication of vision requires communication of meaning.
- Attention should be given to institutionalizing vision if leadership is to be successful.

In much of the literature on educational leadership there is considerable emphasis on vision. However, the strategic dimension of leadership does not consist only of the vision element of leadership ability but also encompasses a far wider range of factors. How can we build a more coherent model of what strategic leadership entails? To answer this question the chapter draws on data from the NCSL research project.

Strategic leadership: findings from the research

In analysing the data from interviews with leaders who have high-level strategic skills, Davies et al. (2005) divided their research findings into what strategic leaders do and what characteristics they possess. The analysis of the data revealed that strategic leaders involve themselves in five key activities in each of two categories as shown in Figure 9.1.

What strategic leaders do

They set the direction of the school

This activity of strategic leaders relates back to traditional definitions of strategy as the pattern of decisions that sets the direction of the organization. Freedman (2003: 2) provides a useful definition, writing that

What strategic leaders do	The characteristics strategic leaders possess
They set the direction of the school.	They challenge and question - they have a dissatisfaction or restlessness with the present.
They translate strategy into action.	They prioritize their own strategic thinking and learning and build new mental models to frame their own and others' understanding.
They align the people, the organisation and the strategy.	They display strategic wisdom based on a clear value system.
They determine effective strategic intervention points.	They have powerful personal and professional networks.
They develop strategic capabilities within the school.	They have high quality personal and interpersonal skills.

Figure 9.1 *Strategic leadership: actions and characteristics*

'strategy is the framework of choices that determine the nature and direction of the organization'. We argued earlier that this comprised a strategic view of three to five years into the future and beyond, and of the broad major thrust of the school's activities. It steps outside current thinking and develops a medium-term perspective. It also involves a number of planning approaches that build capacity to understand the feasibility of different future possibilities.

Leadership voices from the NCSL study considered their strategic leadership role as:

It is taking a long-term view about what the vision is for the school and then strategy is about how you achieve that vision over a period of time. At the moment we are working with a five-year timescale and I think that is right initially but I don't think we should ever lose sight of the longer term than that.

Your strategy is how you are going to get there, what kind of structures you put in place in the school, what measures you take to make things happen, how you use the money – all these things build up a strategy to getting where you want to get to.

Strategy for me is about having a plan of where you are going and why you are going where you are going.

This strategic direction involves a process of not just looking forward from the present but establishing a strategic picture of what we want the school to look like in the future and setting guidelines and frameworks for how to move forward to that position. Strategic leaders in the NCSL study referred to the strategic conversations with colleagues that reinforce a clear understanding of the direction in which the school is going.

> The leadership development significance of this first point is to develop in ourselves and our colleagues time and opportunities to both formulate and articulate the strategic direction of the school.

They translate strategy into action

Most organizations establish plans but they do not always translate them into action. The NCSL research showed that good strategic leaders were also good 'completer finishers'. In Mintzberg's (2003: 67) terms, they were able not only to 'see ahead' but also to 'see it through'. This is facilitated by the ability of strategic leaders to focus on a limited number of key strategic issues and drive forward on those issues. There is considerable debate in the business world about the extent to which traditional strategic plans ever get implemented. It is often suggested that only 10–30 per cent of all plans are achieved, with the rest never being fulfilled. Davies and Ellison (1999; 2003) make use of the idea that the thicker the plan the less it affects practice. In the educational world do schools' plans merely provide frameworks for external audit or do these get implemented and affect practice? One of the leadership voices from the NCSL research stated:

It's not enough just to do that thinking and reflecting but then people actually want to see results.

The leadership ability of being able to build a sense of purpose and direction for the school but also translate that into reality is a critical skill. One of the leaders in the study commented on the importance of building credibility on smaller strategic changes to establish the credibility for more fundamental change:

> *If you can implement two or three items effectively and the staff can see the benefit they are more likely to work with you when you come to a major change because they can see something will come of it.*

There is a danger that, when strategy is seen as a desirable activity, an enormous amount of time is spent designing strategic frameworks and plans. The question should always be, how does this affect practice? How do we translate the framework into the capacity to move towards outcomes that benefit the school? There is a need to continue to have the strategic vision with strategic ability to translate the strategic vision into action. Fullan (2004: xiiii) uses the term 'doers with big minds' to describe system thinkers in action. We need the strategic view but we also need leaders who can 'do' the strategy as well as design it.

> The leadership development significance of this is to develop in ourselves and our colleagues the ability to deliver strategic outcomes as well as strategic plans.

They align the people, the organization and the strategy

Building capacity in depth within the school to deliver the strategy is vital. Davies (2003) outlines a four-stage ABCD approach as first, *articulating* the strategy, in oral, written and structural ways; second, *building* a common understanding through shared experiences and images; third, through dialogue, *creating* a shared mental map of the future and, fourth, *defining* desired outcomes. These processes build a powerful understanding within the staff to enable them to contribute fully to strategic implementation. Novak (2002) talks about the difference in strategic change of 'doing to' staff in the organization and as a result very often 'doing them in'. He argues passionately for an approach of 'doing with' as a way of building long-term commitment to change. Leadership voices from the NCSL study articulate the need to move from a top-down approach to encompass wider leadership:

> *The strategic view for me was about it actually being owned by more people. I think when I started out as a headteacher I felt very much the strategy was mine. I soon realized that it needed to be shared and built by a wide group of people if it was to be implemented in a sustainable way.*

I think it's all about sustainability and what you have to do – in fact leadership is about creating a culture within the school where everyone shares the responsibility for building the future.

Strategic leaders pay a great deal of attention to building a sustainable strategy that develops and involves all those who work in the school. Traditional management approaches suggest aligning the staff to the strategy but it may be better to think of empowered organizations that align the people, the organization and the strategy together.

> The significance of this for leadership development is to seek alignment as a three-way process of people, organization and strategy, and develop in ourselves and our colleagues the ability to build a strategic approach.

They determine effective strategic intervention points

The strategic leadership challenge of when to make a change can be as significant as what change to make. This is a critical issue of timing which can arise from both a rational analysis but also from leadership intuition (Parikh, 1994). There is a useful distinction between 'Chronos' time and 'Kairos' time (Bartunek and Necochea, 2000). The former is the normal ticking of the clock and the passage of time; the latter points to those intense moments in time when critical actions and decisions take place. There are critical points at which strategic leaders can make successful interventions. Strategic leaders in the Davies et al. (2005) research appreciated the importance of strategic timing. If leaders waited until all staff were 'onside' then the opportunity to change may well have passed by. If leaders move too quickly, without support, the change may flounder. Judging when both external circumstances and internal conditions can be managed to effect successful change is a significant ability. Leaders in the research project commented:

So you have to decide where you want to go and seize the opportunity and build capacity within the school.

You have to pick the right moment but also be careful that you don't wait for every single detail to be in place.

I learnt very early on to spend as much time on how *you implement as to* what *you implement and I spend a lot of time on what is the best way to do it.*

As important as strategic timing is the concept of strategic abandonment. This can be defined as the ability to give up or abandon some activities to create the capacity to undertake the new activity. The difference between abandoning things that are not working well and abandoning those that are satisfactory because there are better ideas to pursue, was articulated by school leaders in the study as:

> I mean I see abandonment as being two different issues really. One is the abandonment of things that are not working and actually taking people's time and energy and you're flogging a dead horse. That's easy to do. The other side of it which I did several times was to actually say OK this is working well and we are really comfortable with it and it's getting the results we want, but actually there is another strategy here that takes us onto the next stage but we can't run them both together. This has to be suspended or abandoned in order to give the other one time to grow.

> But the challenge for me personally is this idea of abandonment that if we take on these initiatives you have so many things you can do but you have to put some on one side or put some off even though they are good things because others are more important.

> In considering what things we might do we also have to consider what we are going to stop doing. And it may be that we will stop doing to make space for something else. It may be we stop doing them because we are not doing it very well anyway, it may be that we have stopped doing something because we have even better things to do.

The key ability of strategic leaders is knowing when to make a change but also how to free up organizational space to have the capacity usefully to move into the new strategic direction.

> The significance of this for leadership development is understanding how to recognize the critical point at which to make a change and the ability to prioritize and abandon less important or unsuccessful activities in favour of new initiatives.

They develop strategic capabilities in the school

This is the concept articulated by Prahalad and Hamel (1990) as 'core competencies' and by Stalk et al. (1992) as 'strategic capabilities'. They relate to fundamental attributes within the school. An example of a longer-term competency would be a fundamental understanding of learning and differentiated needs of children. This could be compared with the more shallow understanding of the latest curriculum initiative from government. Leaders in the study focused on developing the longer-term abilities. A useful analogy here is that of a tree (as discussed in Chapter 8). Above the surface are the things that can be seen, such as the trunk and the branches, and below the surface are the roots that hold everything together. Leaders can develop skills (the above-the-surface things) such as how to manage the latest initiative or assessment procedure, but these are current skills. If leaders develop strategic capabilities or strategic competencies, these would be different in depth and range. There would be a reflective learning culture in the staff, a no-blame problem-solving teamwork approach and a deep understanding, for example, of learning and differentiation. When the school faces new challenges it would be able to draw on this reservoir of abilities and not have to rely on current skills. Leaders in the study commented:

> *Instead of doing what we always do, the strategic capability I want is to 'challenge the status quo' and always ask – why, not just how, but why – why are we doing it like that, and then how can we do it differently.*

> *Many of my staff are very good knowers but they are not learners. I want to develop a learning culture and learning about learning culture.*

> *We have a research and development team – they go out and about looking for new ideas. We need to be underpinned in our daily activities with reflecting on what could be different.*

Strategic leaders have the capacity to both manage the 'now' of school life but also the ability to allocate time and resources to build strategic capabilities to ensure the school will be sustainable and develop in the longer term.

The significance of this for leadership development is to build long-term capacity to develop strategic capabilities and not just short-term skills.

What characteristics strategic leaders display

The aspect of strategic leadership found in the Davies et al. (2005) research related to the personal characteristics of school leaders in their study. They found that the leaders displayed five main characteristics:

They challenge and question – they have a dissatisfaction or restlessness with the present

One of the driving forces behind strategic leaders is that they see that the organization can perform in different ways in the future. They want to challenge the current situation and improve things in the future. This means they have to deal with the ambiguity of not being satisfied with present arrangements and at the same time not being able to change things as quickly as they might want. One leader in the NCSL study commented:

> *Part of the problem has been that, in some people's eyes, we were already successful. Why, then, change a winning formula? Some were content with the way things were, they were comfortable with existing strategies because they appeared to be working. But I knew we could do different and better things.*

Leaders are change agents within their organization. They constantly ask questions such as:

- What are the things that we teach that have been clearly successful or unsuccessful in the past? What accounted for the success or otherwise? What do we need to do in the future that is different?
- Which relationships with students, parents and the wider education system have been particularly successful or unsuccessful, and why? What can we do to change things for the better?
- How can we fundamentally review what we do to challenge the current pattern of understanding and operation?
- As a school are we cruising and strolling or are we challenging and creating?

As we saw in Chapter 2, Collins (2001) looks at five levels of leadership. The highest level, level 5, has leaders who are personally modest but are ambitious for their organizations and challenge average performance. Collins articulates one of the characteristics of level-5 leaders as 'demonstrating an unwavering resolve to do whatever must be done to produce the best long-term results, no matter how difficult' (ibid.: 36). While this seems straightforward, it is in fact very complex in that managing the ambiguity of the current situation while driving towards long-term goals requires high-level leadership skills.

> The significance of this for leadership development is that the strategic leader must manage the dissonance of current restlessness and dissatisfaction, while driving for significant change in the future.

They prioritize their own strategic thinking and learning, and build new mental models to frame their own and others' understanding
This is a significant characteristic of strategic leaders. To envision the future in order to develop new approaches requires both knowledge and experience. Strategic leaders in the study were very aware of their learning needs and prioritized time to meet those. They were also seekers after new experiences to broaden their repertoire of skills. New challenges need new skills, and the leaders in the study saw continuous professional development as a means of achieving those skills. They framed their new understandings in mental models which they used in communication with other staff. Coble (2005: 41) makes a powerful point:

> *those who are able to stay on track and avoid derailment are leaders who have become perpetual learners. Not only do they learn more from their experience than those who derail, but they are also able to figure out how they are learning from their experiences so that they are able to learn more and more and at faster rates.*

The need for leaders to be active learners to develop and enhance their existing skills seems both desirable and necessary. It is currently said that heads in schools should change their title from headteacher to 'lead learner' to emphasize the importance both of leaders being active learners themselves and of modelling good practice for others in the organization. The difficulty for leaders is that they have very busy lives and prioritizing time for themselves to the exclusion of other tasks is one that many leaders find difficult. Schön (1987) makes a distinction between reflection-on-action and reflection-in-action. This is worth serious consideration as developing the skills to develop reflection-in-action can build the capacity to determine learning needs and build frameworks to meet them. Leaders in the NCSL study commented:

I need to get away from the school to attend conferences both to learn new things and to step back and try and see the whole picture of what we are doing and what we should be doing.

If I have to explain it to other people I need to understand it in depth and that means time for reflection.

I set aside time each week, with the team, to look at strategic issues separated out from the day-to-day detail.

Mental models can be considered to be pictures or frameworks to capture reality, which is often complex and rapidly changing. Leaders make sense of reality for themselves and their staff by creating these frameworks as a means of more clearly interpreting the world. The point of engaging in this process is that it enables all those working in the school to share a common meaning or understanding and it builds a common purpose.

> The significance of this for leadership development is that leaders need to develop their own learning and understanding as much as they focus on the learning and understanding of students in their care.

They display strategic wisdom based on a clear value system
The earlier definition of strategic leadership in Chapter 2 (Figure 2.2) showed it as linking values and vision with operational matters. Having a clear value system which is ethically based was seen by the leaders in the study as the bedrock for all their activities. The wisdom to make the 'best' decisions was based not just on a good understanding of what change was possible, but also what was in the best interest of the children. The leaders in the study used a series of value statements in their interaction with colleagues to set the framework for their strategic decisions. One leader in the NCSL study commented:

I have developed a series of leadership questions I ask staff to give them and me time to understand the nature of what we are doing and give us time to understand what might be the wisest choice such as 'What is in the best interest of the children?' or 'What choices do we have?' or 'Who will benefit and who will not benefit?'

The defining of core values or a set of beliefs is vital in this process as it provides the bedrock on which to base critical decisions.

Wisdom may be defined as the capacity to take the right action at the right time. In a presentation to the 2002 International Thinking Skills Conference, Robert Sternberg articulated that leaders need wisdom because they:

- need creative abilities to come up with ideas;
- need analytical abilities to decide whether the ideas are good ideas;
- need practical abilities to make their ideas functional and to convince others of the value of their ideas;
- need wisdom to balance the effects of ideas on themselves, others and institutions in both the short and long run.

In addressing the nature of wisdom in more depth he established that wisdom is:

- successful intelligence;
- balancing of interests;
- balancing of time frames;
- mindful infusion of values;
- aligning of responses to the environment;
- application of knowledge for the common good.

He further established that for successful intelligence there is a need to combine practical intelligence, analytical intelligence and emotional intelligence. This provides an insightful and challenging set of ideas for leaders to develop their personal set of skills and abilities to deploy strategic choices with wisdom and effectiveness.

> The significance of this for leadership development is that building the capacity to reflect on taking the right action at the right time is not easy and that leaders need to develop reflective practice to enhance their skills in this area.

They have powerful personal and professional networks

Knowledge, as we saw earlier, is a critical factor in forming strategic decisions. Networks of fellow professionals and organizations that were local, regional, national and international were seen as the fundamental way to gain both new understanding and to benchmark their current understanding. The NCSL research showed that strategic leaders put a great deal of time and effort into maintaining and extending their networks. The significance of networks is supported by Fullan (2004: 17) who states 'if you want to change systems, you need to increase the amount of purposeful interaction between and among individuals … and indeed within and across systems'.

Leaders need to place a high level of importance on developing extensive networks to provide them with the insights to fulfil the complexities of their post. Many organizations provide introductions to powerful networks. It is the drive and the enthusiasm of the leaders both to utilize these formal organizational networks and to build on top of those their own personal professional networks that provide them with the professional knowledge they need.

One of the leaders in the NCSL study commented:

Networks, networks, networks … I have learnt that I need multiple information and support networks to do my job. The rapid pace of change means I have to constantly share ideas with colleague to make sense of what is happening.

> The significance of this for leadership development is that building a wide and deep information and support network has become increasingly important in developing strategic capacity in the leadership of schools.

They have high-quality personal and interpersonal skills

In Chapter 6 we saw one definition of leadership as 'getting things done with people', this was very evident in the NCSL study. Leaders in the research talked about building greater personal understanding of how to increase their own confidence and resilience as well as understanding others on the school staff. Honest relationships and making time to listen to others were seen as the cornerstones of strategic efforts led by school leaders. One leader in the study reported:

I am constantly trying to listen and support people to really understand where they are coming from. They need to trust and believe me and feel I am working in their best interests.

Throughout the discussion about wisdom (see page 115), the personal qualities of leaders have been highlighted. Central to these qualities are the values they hold. Translating wisdom into action requires the ability to inspire and stimulate, social intelligence, the ability to be passionate. All these qualities affect the way a leader learns and is able to change. Boal and Hooijberg (2001: 532) suggest that 'most leadership researchers agree that leaders need to have important interpersonal skills such as empathy, motivation, and communication'. Bennett (2000: 3) expands the importance of personal values:

If moral leadership is to be exercised and pedagogy re-engineered with any degree of success, then future leaders will need a firm set of personal values. No doubt many will have their own lists, but integrity, social justice, humanity, respect, loyalty and a sharp distinction between right and wrong, will all need to be included. Strategic relationships will soon flounder unless such a value system is held with conviction and exercised on a regular consistent basis.

Although not specifically included in Bennett's comprehensive list, social intelligence is important for strategic leadership because the process of decision-making, solution implementation and organizational improvement is rarely free of emotion. Interpersonal intelligence includes having a thorough understanding of the social context, and is defined by Gardner (1985: 239) as the ability 'to notice and make distinctions among other individuals … in particular among their moods, temperaments, motivations and intentions'. So a key component of social intelligence is the ability to discern emotion both in oneself and in others. Gardner identifies this as both intrapersonal and interpersonal intelligence. The ability to connect the involvement of others and to resolve conflicts will be increasingly vital in a context of developing strategic relationships and finding creative solutions. Bennett (2000: 4) also identifies the importance of strength and courage: 'visionary projects, delivered with passion, will fail unless the leader has the ability to counter adversaries and remain confident until the conclusion has been reached'.

The significance of this for leadership development is that strategic leadership becomes effective only if we empower and create a sense of meaning for colleagues. Thus our skills in working with others need to be constantly improved and developed.

Conclusion – creating a model for strategic leadership

The challenge for schools is always to manage the now effectively but also to develop improved and innovative frameworks for the future. A key approach to developing a more strategic orientation in the school is to enhance the strategic leadership capability in both the senior leadership team and a wider group of staff who provide leadership in wider areas of the school. B. Davies and B.J. Davies (2005) build on a model created by B.J. Davies (2004). This takes as its centre point developing a leader's strategic wisdom, and can be seen in Figure 9.2.

The model argues that an individual leader's strategic intelligence is made up of three wisdoms: people wisdom, contextual wisdom and procedural wisdom. The successful deployment of these three wisdoms is what makes up successful strategic leadership.

People wisdom, as the name suggests, is concerned with the skills required to interact successfully with people in the school and the wider school community. It involves intrapersonal and interpersonal skills, the ability to understand ourselves and others as a cornerstone of all other behaviours; these behaviours provide a basis for the four enhancement activities. These are: enhancing participation, enhancing motivation, enhancing capability and enhancing competencies. The purpose of enhancing *participation* is to increase the involvement of others in the strategic process. This increased involvement through participation should result in enhanced *motivation* of the individuals in the school. The aim of this enhanced participation and motivation is twofold: first, to increase the level of involvement and commitment and, second, to enhance capability and competencies in the organization. *Capability* can be seen as the ability to do the current job, while *competencies* are the generic skills those leaders bring to the challenge of leadership to solve problems by working with others.

Contextual wisdom concerns both an awareness of and an understanding of the organizational and environmental context in which the leader operates. One of the most difficult challenges of leaders is both to understand and then positively develop the culture of a school. The significance of beliefs and values in promoting a positive strategic future for the school cannot be underestimated. The underlying assumptions about the nature of children and their potential achievements, how we work together, the levels of trust, the role of parents and the community are grounded in a series of beliefs and values. It is

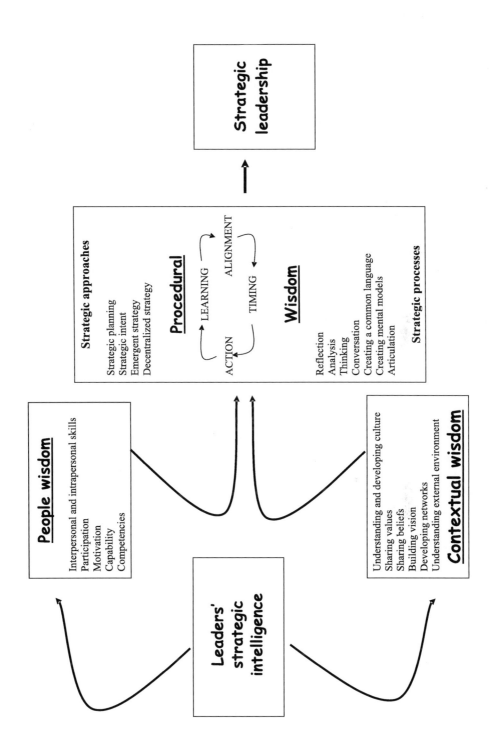

Figure 9.2 *A model for strategic leadership (Davies, B.J., 2004: 162)*

first necessary to understand the values and beliefs and then, if necessary, change and develop them. Strategic leaders understand the importance of these beliefs and values as they are critical to building a vision of how the school is going to develop. Insights on developing the school are not just built on an understanding of internal factors; they are also predicated on powerful personal and professional networks. These networks assist in interpreting and understanding the wider external environment in which the school operates.

Procedural wisdom links the two previous wisdoms. Understanding the people and understanding the context are vital leadership abilities, but in themselves they have little value unless that understanding can result in something getting done! This is the significance of procedural wisdom. There are three elements to procedural wisdom. The first is strategic approaches. These provide the understanding of different ways to deploy a strategic approach, those of strategic planning, strategic intent, emergent strategy and decentralized strategy. These strategic approaches need to be deployed alongside a fundamental understanding of the second element of strategic processes. The key element of the processes are conceptualizing, engaging the people, articulation and implementation (see Davies et al. 2005).

The interrelationship between strategic approaches and strategic processes operates through a third element, which is made up of a four-stage process of learning, alignment, timing and action, as seen in Figure 9.3

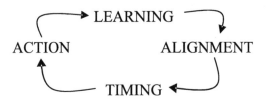

Figure 9.3 *The procedural wisdom cycle*

Learning about the nature of strategy and the approaches and processes that can be utilized leads to aligning the people, the organization and the strategy to form a coherent view of where the school is going. When to move and implement the strategy is dependent on strategic timing, and strategic timing is demonstrated by knowing when the best strategic intervention point is in place. When the right time has been decided then strategic action can take place. Learning the lessons of that action starts the cycle operating again.

Strategic leadership has often been seen to be the role of the single leader. This chapter has initially attempted to consider what strategic leaders do and the characteristics they possess. It has drawn, in Figure 9.2 a model of strategic leadership. This is a significant model for leaders to reflect on their strategic abilities and how they develop those abilities in others. Understanding the people (people wisdom) and understanding the context (contextual wisdom) is a prerequisite for moving on to the strategic processes and strategic approaches. However, strategy is a dynamic process and current knowledge of process and approaches will be insufficient for the long-term development of the leader. Leaders must be 'lead learners' in their organization. The priority the model gives to procedural wisdom where both leaders and their organizations operate a cycle of learning, alignment, timing and action and back to learning is critical. We saw earlier in the characteristics of strategic leaders that they are restless and challenge and question the existing shape and direction of their organization. They also combine this with prioritizing their own learning. Developing strategic leadership is a journey that the model in this chapter provides in a framework for strategic development.

By analysing the nature and dimensions of strategic leadership it is hoped this will form the basis for discussing in leadership teams how they can develop their strategic skills and share those skills with wider groups within the staff.

Chapter 10

Deploying and implementing strategy

Introduction

So far the book has considered, based on a value and belief system, the various processes and the various approaches that can be deployed in building a strategically focused school. The book has also considered the nature and dimensions of strategic leadership which drive both processes and approaches. In this chapter we bring processes and approaches, together with the strategic leadership, into a holistic view of implementing a strategy in a school setting. This chapter revises existing ideas already established in the book, and introduces new ideas to examine how individual strategies can be implemented. The chapter also looks at how a more holistic cross-organizational view can be obtained by using a strategic map. My warning is that it is one thing to have strategic intents or plans, it is another to implement them successfully!

Consider the story of three frogs on a lily pad (Figure 10.1): one frog decides to jump off – how many are left? The answer is three; deciding to do something and actually doing something are very different. A school may have eloquently written plans which do not come to fruition. It is important to consider how any strategic approach can be translated effectively into action. This chapter is organized into three aspects of implementation: basic factors, people factors and organizational factors.

What strategic implementation strategy should do

The implementation process should aim to work back from a vision of the future and create a strategy that is action orientated and deliver specific strategic outcomes. How can this be achieved when the majority of strategic plans never come to fruition? To answer this question this chapter considers three factors, previously mentioned, when implementing strategy: basic factors, people factors and organizational factors. Using these three factors it is hoped to provide the reader with insights into his/her own strategy for organizational reality and success. To start the discussion of translating strategy into action we shall consider two underlying basic factors that are critical for success.

Figure 10.1 *Translating strategy into action*

Implementation – basic factors

The two basic factors that are paramount are:

- focus on a few themes which will make a real difference;
- keep the process simple.

These two criteria seem obvious but are, in fact, often neglected. Freedman (2003: 18) states: 'Strategy is based around the answers to a few vital questions, rather than masses of data.' Using that concept we should ask what the few vital questions initially are in implementation? We saw in Chapter 8, in considering strategic intent statements and strategic plans, that readers were advised not to follow the detailed structures and lists of school development/improvement plans, but instead to look at a maximum of five strategic areas for development. This advice needs to be repeated. What are the key things that will make a difference? In terms of implementation what are the critical factors that will lead to successful implementation? There are always many activities and conversations that leaders can engage in with their colleagues to decide which are critical to lead to successful implementation. The three things that lead to successful implementation are focus, focus and focus!

This means that leaders need to develop both good content questions and good process questions. Working with colleagues, leaders need to define critical areas for strategic development and then take sufficient time to outline the nature and dimensions of the proposed strategic change, so that a complete picture of the critical factors for implementation can be built up. The other side of the coin to 'what we are doing?' is 'how we are doing it?' Here leaders need to understand the how of implementation. This involves a process of determining the key factors that need to be communicated in order to gain commitment of colleagues. I suggest that commitment will be more effective if leaders can identify the main elements of the change but also the main implementation points and the possible problems that may arise.

As well as keeping the focus, keeping the implementation process simple is an important contributor to success. This involves both defining and articulating the key stages and sign points of the implementation strategy. Planning the implementation is as important as planning the content of the strategy itself. Clarity of process and establishing definable outcomes along the way are key elements to build into the overall approach. Given that leadership and management involves working with and through people, the people dimension is analysed next.

Implementation – people factors

In this section I consider four implementation actions which involve people. First, there is a need to align the people, the organization and the strategy. This is to ensure that everyone is working in the same direction. Second, there is a need to ensure that strategy is not seen as the role of the single leader but work towards making strategy everyone's job. Thus people at all levels of the organization should be involved in the design, implementation and articulation of the strategy. Third, strategy should not be seen as a one-off process, with the strategic planning process taking place once a year, but as an ongoing developmental process. Fourth, if strategy is to be successful it will need effective leadership and if there is to be strategic change then leadership will play a critical role. The chapter now looks at these four factors in more detail.

Align the people, the organization and the strategy

This is the difficult task of moving the individual and corporate 'mind-set' to the strategic objectives of the organization.

Kouzes and Posner (1999: xv) put forward the view that:

> *Leaders create relationships, and one of those relationships is between individuals and their work. Ultimately we all work for a purpose, and that purpose has to be served if we are to feel encouraged. Encouraging the heart only works if there's a fit between the person, the work and the organization.*

Gratton (2000) sees three core capabilities to make these relationships happen: emotional capability, trust-building capability and the capability to build a psychological contract. Emotional capability involves the organization building a climate to link individual needs with organizational needs and developing a sustainable environment. Trust links to the values and beliefs identified in Chapter 3. Do staff see the interactions in school as both honest and fair? Do staff believe leaders in the organization have the skills to take the organization forward in a successful and sustainable way? Trust is the bedrock on which inspiration and commitment can be built. The psychological contract is when individuals agree with the school's purpose and way of working, and can commit to 'going the extra mile' for a set of beliefs which can be turned into action. Leaders in the NCSL study commented:

> *It's about us and not the old thing of 'oh well it's what the senior leadership team want', or 'oh it's about what someone else wants', or 'it's an external imposition' – it's now actually about what we want.*

> *We are articulating clearly our intents and I guess the stage that we are going into now is a sense of alignment where I can align the desires of the staff, the parents and the governors to move the school forward in the coming five to ten years.*

These comments from leaders in the study highlight that the challenge in most organizations is to reconcile organizational and individual perspectives. The processes of involving staff in being part of the organization's values and direction are critical. How individuals come to believe in what the school is doing and can articulate broader school aims, as well as their individual targets, is a key feature of alignment. Thus, with the importance of strategy in its guiding role in the school, staff have to both understand the strategy as well as commit to it. The challenge of aligning individuals and the organization was highlighted many times in the study.

Making strategy everyone's job

Strategy should be seen as influencing current behaviour but also as a source of dialogue to build future behaviour.

This involves more than compliance on behalf of the staff. Kouzes and Posner (1999: xv) see this as about a discussion on the 'soul and spirit in the workplace' Gratton (2000: 19–20) sees this as 'engaging with the soul of the organisation'. Building on trust and commitment means involving everyone in the organization in the strategic journey. This involves building a highly committed workforce with creative teams to support a culture of innovation within the school. Leaders in the NCSL study made the following observations:

> *The strategic view for me was about actually being owned by more people. When I started out as a head, I think I felt very much it was mine, and then after about a year or so, I felt I shared it with the senior team, and they owned it and from years three through to six I would say definitely that it had filtered down to middle leaders and I think they began to embrace the school culture. The school culture began to be more strategic as a result of that.*

> *We are trying to involve as wide a group of people as possible. We need to share, and have everyone believe in what we are doing, so that together we can build a better future. It is emotional as well as a rational process.*

These comments show the significance of building a deep-seated understanding of the strategic direction held by a wide cross-section of the staff and that this is a key component of successful implementation. The hopes and directions of the school can only be fully realized if everyone in the school takes responsibility for the strategy.

Make strategy a continual process

Strategy should not be articulated and then left, it should be a process of continual review and development.

One of the traditional views of strategy is that leaders write a five-year plan and at the end of the five years write another one. Nothing could be further from good practice! Strategic plans and strategic intent frameworks need to be articulated over a three to five year time frame but they should be seen as flexible documents able to be adjusted and amended when new ideas and information become available. Strategy should be seen as a framework that is constantly under review. Two of the leaders in the NCSL study commented:

> *We have avoided the trap of writing a plan and then next year writing a new one. We are revising and updating at key moments so that it is a living document.*

> *Our plan is a framework that we adapt as we go along.*

This should not mean that the school is rewriting its planning framework every day! What it does mean is that, after the planning framework has been established, if significant developments arise the plans should be revised and adapted. They should be seen as documents that guide action and not something that is filled in once a year and left. This is even more important when it comes to the discussions and strategic conversations that take place. These should form the basis of ongoing discussions and strategic conversations.

Mobilize strategic change through effective leadership

Leaders have to lead by example and demonstrate commitment to the strategy.

Leaders deal with the complexity of creating consistent meaning both for and within the organization. What senior leaders say and, probably more importantly, how they behave, will set the framework for strategic dialogue and strategic action within the school. It is important that leaders understand the values and norms of the school and live out these values in the interactions they have with colleagues. They also face the challenge of understanding the history of the school and where it has come from while being passionate advocates for strategic change. They need to be the voice of support for others involved in the change process. As schools change, leaders need to ensure that core meaning and purpose are not lost but are conceptualized in the new context and is articulated by others.

A leader in the NCSL study commented:

I think it's all about sustainability and what you have to do – in fact leadership is about creating a culture within the school where everyone buys into the responsibility for leadership but you have to live it and believe in it to set the model of commitment.

This ability to live the strategy and convey its importance to others not only in what is written down but also in what the leader says and does is a critical component of effective implementation. Mobilizing effective strategic change is one of the key responsibilities of leaders in organizations.

Implementation – organizational factors

In implementing strategy, from an organizational perspective, four factors need to be considered: first, how strategy can be translated into operational activities and become action; second, how strategy can be developed either in a sequential or parallel fashion; third, when to make a strategic change and what to give up in making capacity for the change, are the concepts of strategy timing and abandonment; and fourth, how the implementation process can make use of strategic maps and balanced scorecards to link individual strategic changes into an overall strategic picture. The chapter now looks at each of these in turn.

Translating strategy into action

The ability to translate the overall broader strategic aims into shorter-term activities over a period of time is the crux of translating strategy into action. The central point here is to ensure that broad strategic aims can be seen to be affecting classroom practice. One way of thinking about this is to consider how strategy can be 'witnessed' as happening in the operational domain. Figure 10.2 shows how three broad strategic aims have been set. By breaking down one of them into its component parts it can be seen how strategy translates into operational activities. Thus a strategic area of development such as 'Leadership and management' may break down into four strategic areas, such as school improvement planning, shared leadership, monitoring and evaluation, and resources and building. By taking one of these at the operational level, that of 'shared leadership skills', it is possible to again break this down into three areas. Looking at one of those area, that of 'develop subject leadership skills', we could consider how we would witness subject leaders adopting the strategic objective. Figure 10.2 suggests that if we look at how the subject leaders are involved in classroom observation, monitoring standards, and how they undertake work scrutiny of pupils' work and how they use data for improvement, we would be able to witness strategy effecting individual practice. Figure 10.2 shows the flow of strategic objectives into operational action. School leaders need to be able to draw up strategic plans and frameworks and ensure they are translated into action. This needs to be given priority and mapped out to ensure success.

Adopting a sequential or parallel approach

Often in models of leadership, the development of leaders is seen as being hierarchical. I wrote an analysis of this in Davies (2003) which is adapted in the following text. Marsh (2000) articulates a sequential linear process ascending through three stages: administration, management and, finally, leadership. These stages assume that there is first the development of administrative skills, then management skills and, finally, leadership skills. Indeed, the NCSL (2001) five levels of leadership development is a sequential process identifying the levels of emergent leadership, established leadership, entry to headship, advanced leadership and consultant leadership. Is this the same with strategy? Do leaders first do the straightforward managerial adjustments and, when they gain confidence, move on to more complex and radical change. This could be considered a sequential view of strategic development. While some, or even the majority of, leaders may adopt this approach, the NCSL research project identifies that strategically orientated leaders

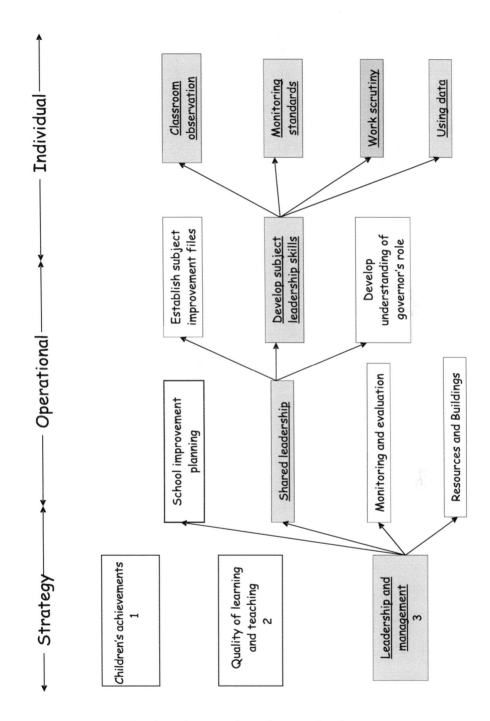

Figure 10.2 *Moving from the strategic to the operational*

do not work in this way. These strategic leaders operated a twin-track strategy. They work both at significantly improving and extending the life of existing approaches and strategies, while at the same time building capability and capacity to move to a significantly enhanced level of operation. This we would call making the strategic leap or bridging the s-curve gap. In considering what strategic leaders do, we can see that this consists of improving what we already do but, significantly, moving to a much higher level of performance. In an outstanding piece of analysis and conceptualization, Mike Jeans (a management consultant and former KMPG consultant) develops the ideas behind the sigmoid curve with a chapter 'Bridging the s-curve gap' (Jeans, 1998).

Many readers will be familiar with the s-curve or sigmoid curve (see Figure 10.3). It suggests that organizations go through a process of growth, success and eventual decline. The axes represent organizational improvement (vertical) and time (horizontal). The analysis suggests that at point A the organization has been successful and should reconsider its operation and reflect on what it needs to do to get on to the next and higher curve. It can either continue as it is and decline to B or move on to the higher curve C.

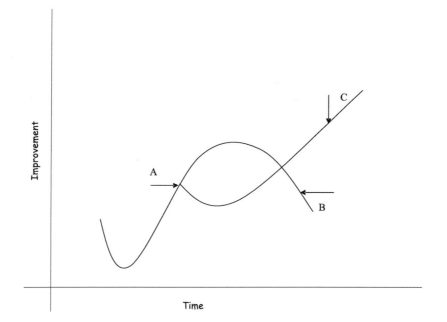

Figure 10.3 *The sigmoid curve (adapted from Handy, 1994: 5 and Jeans, 1998: 24)*

Jeans (1998) puts forward a significant development (in Figure 10.4) on this analysis. He suggests that organizational leaders attempt to do two things. First, they try to significantly improve the existing way of operating. In doing so they intend to stop the curve flattening and to elongate it. While doing so they also develop capability to shift to a whole new way of operating, at a much higher level. This can be called the strategic leap (see Figure 10.4). He gives this very valuable insight from the business world:

> *When Midland Bank (now part of HSBC) decided in the late 1980s to set up a telephone banking operation, it did so by creating a separate organisation, First Direct. This was arguably a second-curve operation, bearing little resemblance to Midland Bank's existing traditional branch banking operation. This did not, however, mean that the latter was ignored. Indeed Midland engaged in a great many first-curve initiatives, such as branch closure/amalgamation or staff reduction to elongate the life of the operation. (Jeans, 1998: 126)*

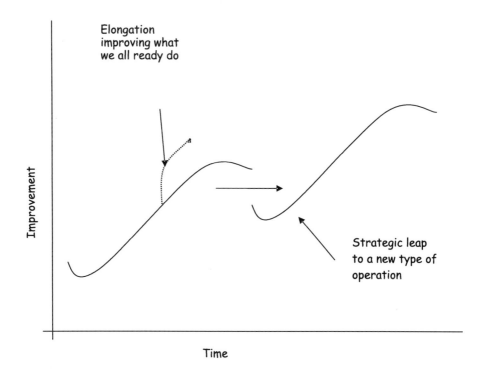

Figure 10.4: *Elongating the s-curve and making the strategic leap (Jeans, 1998)*

In the education sector, I have been privileged to work with Greg Barker and Derek Wise, outstanding headteachers from the primary and secondary sectors respectively. In a series of strategic conversations with them, we discussed how they both focused on improving the current way of operating (elongating the sigmoid curve) and preparing the ground for a strategic leap to a totally new way of operating. What follows is a case example of how they adopt a twin-track strategy.

Case example: Greg Barker, St Vincent's Primary School

Part of the problem has been that, in some people's eyes, we were already successful. Why, then, change a winning formula? Some were content with the way things were, they were comfortable with existing strategies because they appeared to be working. For some, therefore, there was little motivation to change. So part of the agenda was to improve what we already did to ensure we did not start to peak and go down the sigmoid curve to point B but the other strategic agenda was to reconceptualize how we could operate in a totally new way. As I learnt more and more about whole-brain learning and Howard Gardner's work on multiple intelligences, I became discontented with the existing situation and the task became clear – there would have to be a significant development programme to introduce the staff to this new science of learning and to promote the introduction of accelerated learning techniques. The work of Davies and Ellison (1999) on school planning has helped me to develop a more holistic and more strategic view of school improvement so that, even in the turbulence that schools now find themselves, it is still possible to remain focused on the core purpose of helping our children to become effective life-long learners. Thus from a new perspective of multiple intelligences and accelerated learning, together with Mihaly Csikszentmihalyi's (1990 and 1997) concept of 'Flow', we prepared a staff development programme that would totally re-engineer our concept of learning and how we would structure our learning and teaching process.

Case example: Derek Wise, Cramlington High School

We worked on twin-track strategies. At one level measures to raise the expectations of the staff and the aspirations of the students. In particular we introduced a new timetable (four periods in the morning, two in the afternoon): a new curriculum to go alongside it with staff held accountable for both discipline and results. We also improved the learning environment with carpeted classrooms, improved student toilets and social facilities. We publicly shared examination results and, because the curriculum structure consisted of 90 per cent common core, we were able to compare faculty areas with each other and to ask pointed but essential questions such as why is this faculty/department/member of staff doing better or worse than that faculty/department/member of staff given that they have exactly the same students? With the students we shared data on their progress, set targets and celebrated success wherever we could find it. We established regular reviews of departments, and guidelines for schemes of work and what we considered to be good teaching and learning. At the same time we were aware that we needed to create capacity and capability for significant change – a strategic leap in performance. If we were to be a school where 'learning is our business' we must recognize that learning is a highly individual matter, and students learn in different ways with preferred styles to access and process information. The decision was taken, therefore, to make a leap to our new sigmoid curve by re-engineering the learning process. We adopted the accelerated learning cycle (Smith, 1996) as a framework and planning tool to design lessons. The cycle blends our developing knowledge of neuroscience, motivational theory and cognitive psychology to increase student engagement in learning and their motivation to achieve. To achieve this we set up a research and development group and identified pilot departments to 'make the leap' to new ways of working. Strategic timing was critical; we needed to move when we had enough capacity and capability to make the change.

Considering strategic timing and strategic abandonment

Barbara Davies and I wrote (Davies and Davies, 2005) 'Determining effective intervention points – the right things at the right time'. This still seems a very good summary of the key issues and it is replicated below.

The leadership challenge of *when* to make a significant strategic change is as critical to success as choosing what strategic change to make. The issue of timing can rest on leadership intuition (Parikh, 1994) as much as on rational analysis. When individuals in the organization are ready for change, when the organization needs the change, and when the external constraints and conditions force the change all have to be balanced one against the other. Such judgement is manifested in not only *knowing what* and *knowing how* but also *knowing when* (Boal and Hooijberg, 2001) and, as important, knowing *what not to do* (Kaplan and Norton, 2001). Therefore we could add to this list knowing *what to give up or abandon* in order to create capacity to undertake the new activity. This was illustrated by two school leaders responding in the NSCL project:

> *I wrote a paper and that basically argued that the climate was right for change, there are some issues that need to be changed but if we are going to do it, then it needs to be part of a coherent programme rather than piecemeal. But the challenge for me personally is this idea of abandonment, that if we take on these initiatives and new things come on, I know I have to give some things up.*

> *The strategic timing is absolutely important. It can make or break a school. If you try and do it at the wrong time it could be disastrous.*

Several of the school leaders in the study talked about the critical issue of strategic timing, of getting the time right for change for themselves and others in the school. One school leader also talked about this timing being intuitive:

> *I think from my own point of view a lot goes on fairly intuitively ... I know I can't go down that road because I'm not ready or they are not ready. So timing is so critical.*

Choosing the right time, and saying 'No' if it wasn't the right time was critical for strategic leaders in the study. Getting the timing right for the school community was about being able to choose which external initiatives to implement which would complement the schools' own agenda for improvement. This was clearly illustrated by one school leader:

> *I think you get better at being a strategic leader the further you go along, because there comes a point when you actually develop the capacity to say 'No, we are not going to do that' or 'No, it's irrelevant. We are not going to do it'.*

Strategic timing affects all the people in the school community. If the strategic timing is wrong it can have devastating effects on the school. People will be divided and realizing the strategy will therefore be impossible.

As we have said, in addition to the critical skill of strategic timing, is that of strategic abandonment. If a school adopts a new way of doing things or adopts a new strategic priority how that fits into an already crowded agenda has to be considered. The result is that leaders have to downgrade the importance or abandon existing strategies, not because they are wrong in themselves, but they have become less significant in comparison to new factors. As one school leader said:

> *I see abandonment as being two different issues. One is the abandonment of things that are not working and actually taking people's time and energy. That's easy to do. The other side of it was to actually say OK this is working well and we are really comfortable with it and it is getting the results we want, but actually there is another strategy here that takes us onto the next stage but we can't run them both together. This has to be suspended or abandoned in order to give the other one time to grow.*

This concept of strategic abandonment is a very powerful one. The difficult aspect of strategic abandonment occurs where the school has to give up acceptable current practice to make capacity available for future improved practice.

Creating a strategic map and implementation structure for the school

While it is important to consider, as we have done above, how to implement an individual strategy, it is also necessary to look at reviewing the whole strategic picture. This can focus on how we review the overall strategic implementation process or how an individual strategic implementation affects the wider school strategy. Starting from scratch, I would suggest that leaders might consider the following two ways to build a holistic view of developing a strategically focused school:

1 Map the strategic architecture of the school.
2 Develop a series of implementation activities to align the school to

the new strategic goals or recognize how a proposed change affects the strategic architecture.

We will now consider each of these in more detail.

Map the strategic architecture of a school
It is important for strategic leaders to have a strategic map or framework to guide them in developing the strategic capacity and capability of their school. A useful term for this could be the 'strategic architecture' of the school. Hamel and Prahalad (1994: 118–19) define this as:

> *Strategic architecture is not a detailed plan. It identifies the major capabilities to be built, but doesn't specify exactly how they are to be built. It shows the relative position of the major load-bearing structures, but not the placement of every electrical outlet and doorknob.*

Kaplan and Norton (1996; 2001) have used a strategic tool called the balanced scorecard, which looks at establishing a number of strategic benchmarks for establishing a framework for strategic mapping and implementation. A very perceptive approach along these lines has been used by Jeans (1998), who uses the KMPG global model to create a strategic map. I have adapted this to create a strategic architecture for a school in Figure 10.5.

This can be seen in more detail in Figure 10.6.

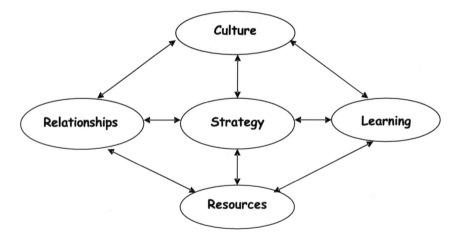

Figure 10.5 *The strategic architecture of the school – overview*

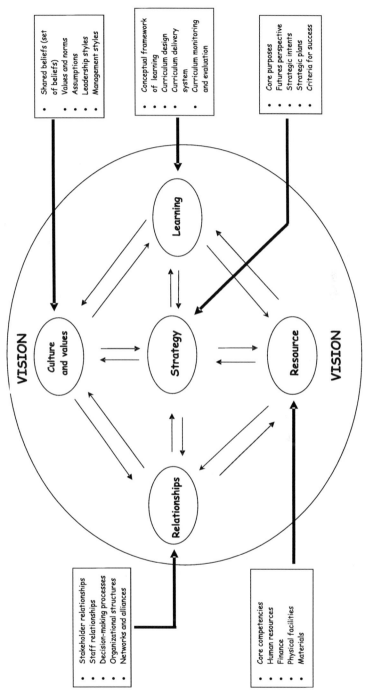

Figure 10.6 *The strategic architecture of the school – detail*

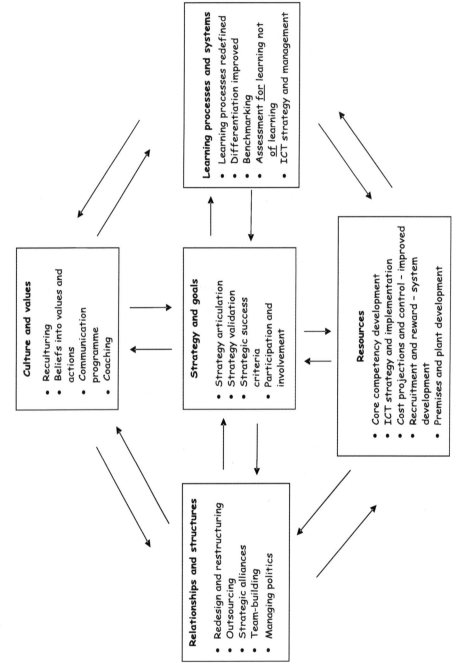

Learning processes and systems

- Learning processes redefined
- Differentiation improved
- Benchmarking
- Assessment <u>for</u> learning not <u>of</u> learning
- ICT strategy and management

Culture and values

- Reculturing
- Beliefs into values and actions
- Communication programme
- Coaching

Strategy and goals

- Strategy articulation
- Strategy validation
- Strategic success criteria
- Participation and involvement

Resources

- Core competency development
- ICT strategy and implementation
- Cost projections and control – improved
- Recruitment and reward – system development
- Premises and plant development

Relationships and structures

- Redesign and restructuring
- Outsourcing
- Strategic alliances
- Team-building
- Managing politics

Figure 10.7 *Strategic activities and processes (adapted from Jeans, 1998: 138)*

*Develop and implement a series of strategic process activities to align the
school to the new strategic goals*
The strategic architecture model provides a strategic leader in a school
with the framework to create a strategic map of the organization. By
examining the elements in each of the five areas of the model, the
leader can assess the existence and relative strengths of the components within each of the five areas. In building a vision of where the
school needs to be in, say, five years' time the leader needs to assess the
gap between the current position and the future position. Turning that
gap into a series of strategic activities can be achieved by adapting Jeans
(1998: 138) 'projects in the organizational systems model' as shown in
Figure 10.7. This shows how using the three implementation factors of
basic, people and organizational might interact with the changes in
each of the five strategy areas.

The significance of this approach is that it provides a series of implementation initiatives and strategies for the school to adopt. It does
bring the different elements of strategic implementation together in
one coherent map of what the school needs to do and how it is doing
it. There is a danger that individual initiative may overlap and conflict.
By having an overview of the strategic implementation structure, leaders in schools can take a holistic view of what is the strategic implementation position of the school

The monitoring and evaluation process is an ongoing one and
should be considered as a feedback loop. It is a process that is incorpo-
rated in the planning frameworks in the strategic intent statements and
strategic plans in Chapter 8. However, it is important to monitor the
pace of implementation and evaluate if all is going according to plan,
or whether alternative approaches are necessary. Monitoring and eval-
uating the implementation stage is a critical factor in ensuring that
strategy turns into action.

Conclusion

Implementation benefits from the idea to 'keep it simple'. To this end
the chapter initially considered the basic factors in implementation
along with 'focus on a few themes that will make a difference'. Then
followed the task of the two challenges of understanding the people
and understanding the organization. In understanding the people
dimension the chapter put forward four ideas: align the people, the

organization and the strategy; make strategy everyone's job; make strategy a continuous people process; mobilize strategic change through effective leadership. The chapter then moved on to look at four organizational factors: translating strategy into action; adopting a sequential or a parallel approach; considering strategic timing and abandonment; and, finally, creating a strategic map and implementation structure for the school.

Strategy is an attractive concept, and plans and documentation abound in school. However, the basic questions to be asked are 'do they ever get implemented?' and 'do they make a difference?' This chapter should be read often as a reminder that implementing a strategy is the key to success and we should not get distracted by more and more elegant strategic designs and documentation and so not spend enough time on implementation and effect. We need to improve the educational opportunities of all our children, and that can only happen if our strategies are implemented.

Chapter 11

A strategically focused school

The fellowship of the nine

Education is a wonderful challenge. The challenge is to give every child the opportunity to learn and develop. We might consider that children are the messages we send into the future. Clearly we need to send good messages. Part of that process is ensuring that we provide high-quality education this week and next term. The other part of that process is building the capacity within the school to ensure that the school is forward-looking and futures orientated to give high-quality education in succeeding years. The purpose of this capacity-building is that as the child develops, the school also needs to adapt and change to meet the challenges of the future. It should become a strategically focused school. Just as the fellowship of the nine set out in *The Lord of the Rings* (Tolkien, 1991: 268) to battle with the forces of Mordor, so I propose nine factors that strategically focused schools should develop and deploy to battle with the dangers of short-termism!

These points are not intended to be prescriptive, nor do I claim that they are all-encompassing, but they seem to me to be issues that school leaders and school staff can use as a basis for their strategic conversations. Strategically focused schools try to:

- develop a culture of sustainability;
- balance the short term and the long term;
- develop strategic measures of success;
- be morally driven;

- focus on learning;
- pay attention to strategic processes;
- pay attention to strategic approaches;
- be part of networked systems;
- develop sustainable strategic leadership across the school.

Develop a culture of sustainability

We saw in Chapter 2 that sustainability is not the same as maintainability and I developed a definition of sustainability as:

> *the ability of individuals and schools to continue to improve to meet new challenges and complexity in a way that does not damage individuals or the wider community but builds capacity and capability to be successful in new and demanding contexts.*

The point about strategy is that it seeks to move the school on from its current situation to a desired and improved future state. In doing so, it needs to ensure that the changes embarked on are not transitory but are embedded within the organization, and will continue as patterns of working. They should not be dependent on a single leader. Initially, the single leader may be the catalyst for the change. However, only if new strategic direction and practices are adopted by wider groups of leaders and staff in the school will they be sustainable. What general principles of sustainability can we bring to the debate about developing a strategically focused school? Hargreaves and Fink (2005: 18) outline seven principles of sustainability; I shall use their perceptive headings as a means of examining what factors need to be present for strategic change to be successful and sustainable. The seven factors are discussed in the following paragraphs.

First is the concept of *depth*. This means that sustainable strategic change must affect the deep and underlying principles of the school's moral purpose and its learning imperative. Sustainable change would focus on developing areas and activities that affect the life opportunities of the children it serves, and the deep learning skills and knowledge that they need to develop. It must also affect all areas of the school. The rhetoric of the values and beliefs contained in documentation of the school needs to be enacted and witnessed in the behaviour and attitudes of children to each other, the behaviour and attitudes of the staff to each other, and the interrelationships between each other. Profound strategic change that lasts must reach down to all aspects of the school's activities and behaviours.

The second concept is that of *length*. By this Hargreaves and Fink mean that strategic change lasts over time. In particular the change is fundamental and desirable, and is not dependent on a single leader. Leadership changes should enhance provision in strategically focused sustainable schools and not result in abandoning one set of practices in favour of the opposite. One primary school I work with has, over more than a decade since the introduction of the national curriculum, resisted a single-subject approach and maintained its integrated cross-curricular topic approach, because the teachers saw that as central to their understanding of learning and their strategic purpose. It was a strategic competency of the school.

The third concept is *breadth*. This is an interesting concept because it means not only spreading new ideas across the staff and students within the school, but in other ways. It certainly means extending the strategic vision, direction and understanding of strategic change across the wider school community of parents and those in the local community. It also means building alliances for strategic change across other schools in the region to support and create a demand for change in the local educational community that will contribute to the long-term enhancement of children's learning opportunities.

Justice is the fourth core concept in sustainable strategic change. This centres on the belief that strategic change should improve the life opportunities of children and the wider community, and it should do so in a way that does not disadvantage others. Thus a school has the responsibility to improve its own institution but it also has a moral obligation to improve education generally within its community. Thus, competing with other schools, rather than co-operating, may sustain the individual school but not the educational community. With the traditional economic dilemma of unlimited wants and limited resources, the way to build sustainable educational communities is through collaboration and developing imaginative resources together. This also links to a later point about being morally driven as such a focus makes a major contribution towards creating social justice.

The fifth concept outlined by Hargreaves and Fink is *cohesive diversity*. They argue 'that strong organizations, too, promote diversity and avoid standardization; in sustainable communities, alignment is an ugly word'. This seems a little idealistic and could underestimate the reality of operating a mass educational system. The argument should be about how frameworks and associated assessments relate to the core skills that children need which will allow them to access the wider curriculum. They should not be seen as an end in themselves. Frameworks need to establish common guidance and expectations and act as a floor to standards. However, excessive testing has made the floor become the ceiling! What we need to do is encourage schools to be more creative in the way they deliver core skills, and allow them greater freedom to develop the curriculum to operate between the floor and ceiling of achievement. A degree of cohesion and of flexibility would more accurately reflect the realities of a mass education system trying to meet individual needs.

The sixth concept is *resourcefulness*. By this I mean that sustainable strategic change is able to enhance and develop its resource base and does not depreciate its physical and human resources. It is increasingly difficult to attract leaders willing to undertake headship roles in schools. When we talk about succession planning usually in terms of preparing individuals for the roles we wish them to undertake, we should also consider the demands the system puts on them to evaluate whether multiple change initiatives makes leadership and management feasible and sustainable in terms of the overload of work and expectations. Leaders have to ensure that the expectations they put on individuals do not wear out their most valuable resource, that of teachers.

Finally, Hargreaves and Fink look at *conservation* in terms of learning from the past to build a better future. There is a dimension of all new government-imposed change where the government believes a new and a fresh start is necessary. 'Excellence and Enjoyment' is a government initiative to replace the dull conformity of the national curriculum in primary schools. However, talk to any primary leader of long-standing, and they will tell you that the overprescriptive national curriculum introduced by the government destroyed much of the integrated theme-based creative curriculum that they once enjoyed! Similarly, the government's spokespeople and leadership gurus are using the buzzwords 'personalized learning' to rethink the curriculum. Actually, most primary schools regard this as good practice, but most of this practice is ignored as the gurus earn their fees by spreading the new cult of personalized learning. Just as we saw earlier, with definitions of strategy, we need to see where we have come from as well as where we are going, in order to build sustainable strategic change.

Balance the short term and the long term

There is an assumption that strategy is about the long term and it is incompatible with short-term objectives. Hargreaves and Fink (2005: 252) make the emphatic statements that:

> *Externally imposed, short-term achievement targets are incompatible with long-term sustainability*

and they go on to say:

> *Imposed, short-term achievement targets (or adequate yearly progress) transgresses every principle of sustained leadership and learning. (Ibid.: 253)*

They set these comments within a powerful disagreement with the work of Michael Fullan:

> *It's particularly important for us to be very clear about one of the most controversial issues in educational reform: targets. Externally imposed, short-term achievement targets are incompatible with long-term sustainability. This is where we part company from our colleague and friend Michael Fullan, with whom we share so many areas of commitment and agreement on leadership, sustainability, and change. Fullan contends, 'The new reality is that governments have to show progress in relation to social priorities ... within one election term [typically four years]. Our knowledge base is such that there is no excuse for failing to design and implement strategies that get short-term results.' (Hargreaves and Fink, 2005: 252)*

I believe Hargreaves and Fink set up a false dichotomy of having short-term results or long-term sustainable improvement but not having both. This, I believe, is inappropriate for a number of reasons. The situation should not be seen as an either/or position. It is of little value trying to convince parents that this year their child has not learnt to read but that 'we have plans in place that may remedy the situation in the next year or two'! The economist John Maynard Keynes was famous for comparing the long- and the short-term perspective by saying that the short-term was important because in the long-term we are all dead! To believe that politicians should not want to see an impact for the money they commit, for the society that pays tax, within an electoral cycle is unrealistic. It is also unrealistic to believe that the government does not want to be guaranteed some basic level of competency by the education system. Most children's experience is short term in relation to what they do this week, this month or what they achieve this year, and which class they are in next year. Success in the short-term is an important factor in their lives, as is success in the long-term.

There are some basic things that an education system should provide for children. It should provide them with definable learning achievements that allow them to function and prosper in society. Where children are not making the progress we expected for them, they need extra support and educational input to help them realize their potential. This, by necessity, needs regular review against benchmarks. Thus Hargreaves and Fink's disdain for 'adequate yearly progress' (2005: 253) is difficult to support. However, I recognize the danger that short-term benchmarks can be seen as the outcomes and not indicators of progress. Indeed, if annual tests were seen as diagnostic and generated learning plans for children rather than outcome scores for schools, the problem of testing may be solved overnight. What needs to be done is that the short term should not be seen as separate from the long term or as in conflict with it, but as part of a holistic framework where short-term assessments are seen as guides on the long-term journey.

This balanced view of the short-term and long-term perspective was shown in Figure 2.1 in Chapter 2 which is replicated in Figure 11.1. It is of little use having a long-term strategic plan if it ignores the short term, as we see in the figure. The result in the bottom-right quadrant will be that short-term crises will prevent the long term ever being achieved. Similarly, merely operating on a short-term perspective, the top-left quadrant, will prevent long-term sustainability ever being achieved. What is needed is a balance between the short and long term as witnessed in the quadrant at the top right.

Short-term planning and short-term assessments are necessary. They are necessary because we live in the short term and need to assess progress. However, the mistake is to plan short term and develop short-

		Functionally successful in the short-term but not sustainable long-term	Successful and sustainable in both the short-term and long-term
Operational processes and planning (SDP and target setting)	Effective		
	Ineffective	Failure inevitable both in the short and long-term	Short-term crises will prevent longer-term sustainability
		Ineffective	**Effective**
		Strategic processes and approaches	

Figure 11.1 *Short-term viability and long-term sustainability (based on Davies, B.J., 2004)*

term targets, and then move on to the longer term. What is necessary is to define moral purpose and the direction of the school, and then to establish a culture that supports long-term development. With the strategic and sustainable direction set, the school can move on to dealing with its shorter-term agenda. It can do this confident that its short-term agenda is set against the longer-term template of sustainability. It should then operate its short-term agenda in line with its longer-term learning and other goals and its value system. Planning backwards is the cornerstone of sustainability. Leaders have to deliver short-term agendas like those demanded by Ofsted reports and SATs results. Good school leaders see these as measures that fit into a larger long-term plan and not as ends in themselves. We should use short-term assessments as diagnostic tools and not as summative outcomes.

The challenge for leaders is to be both leaders and managers. Vision that cannot be translated into action has no impact. Similarly, continuing to manage the now without change and development is not building capacity for the future. We need to balance both the long- and the short-term approaches. Derek Wise, headteacher of Cramlington High School, has a delightful expression to describe himself – a 'prag-matopian'. By this he means he has his head in the clouds to see the future (utopian) but is pragmatic enough to have his feet on the ground to make sure everything is working in the short-term. This balancing of the short term and the long term is a key factor in leading strategically focused schools.

Develop strategic measures of success

What would a strategically focused school look like? How would it know if it was successful in five or seven years' time? One of the ways of answering these two questions would be that a strategically focused school would have established strategic measures of success. One of the useful ideas here is that of how you would witness that success. In setting success criteria, the temptation could be to extend some of the short-term measures of success that are currently used in the league-table culture. However, this would commit two errors. One would be the use of measures of 'shallow' learning, those of easily replicable knowledge, rather than profound or deep learning. The second would be that this approach would be one of planning forward, not utilizing the idea of planning backwards that we discussed earlier. Another challenge is that of measurement. The standard maxim that we 'value what we can measure' rather than 'we measure what we value' is a useful starting point here. It draws into the debate the balance between qualitative and quantitative measures. Results of responses to standardized tests can be reported in a relatively straightforward way. While such results can be indicative of underlying ability, they are only 'indicative'; they do not define deep understanding, motivation to learn or love of the subject area. Other more complex learning, such as social learning, can be witnessed by children's behaviour to each other or towards adults. More complex skills such as problem-solving, determination and commitment became more difficult to assess.

Similar challenges arise when trying to assess the quality and impact of the staff, both on the school as a learning organization, and on the quality of childrens' learning. It would be easy to measure the qualifications of staff or the number of staff development courses they attend, but these could be considered input measures to the organizational capacity of the school. The question that arises from such inputs is, 'Did they make any difference?' Attending courses exposes individuals to new knowledge and skills, but a more difficult set of outcomes to measure is whether they interact with their ideas, reflect on their level of understanding and change behaviours. Returning to the questions of 'What would we want our school to be like in five years' time?' and 'How would we witness what would be happening?' links to the concept of strategic intents that we looked at in Chapter 5. This is more akin to setting desired outcomes and objectives that could be achieved by changing the behaviours and deep-seated culture of the school. Let us now look at some of the strategic measures of success for the school in terms of its students, its staff and the wider community.

The core strategic measure of success would be to create active involvement in sustainable learning for each child. This would start with valuing learning within the school community, but significantly, each child would recognize the need to see learning as an ongoing process throughout his/her life. The current concern in the UK, and many westernized countries, regarding the increase in obesity in children and in adults and the lack of sensible exercise and diet undertaken is a case in point. The obsession in the USA with team sports and competitive sports, and to a degree the culture of team sports in UK schools, has set up a culture of reward and success for the few and humiliation for the rest. The success criterion for secondary school sport may not be 'Did the hockey or football team win the cup?' but 'How many children are actively engaged in physical exercise five years after they have left school?' I would hazard a guess at less than a quarter, and that could be an overestimate!

So strategic measures of success might be some of the following:

- all students engaged in sport, not just the elite teams;
- students are engaged in physical activity several years after they have left school;
- staff are reflective practitioners – they stay after school and discuss ideas with colleagues and build professional learning communities;
- there is a 'no blame culture' where individuals try new things and learn from their mistakes;
- absenteeism for staff and students decreases – because they like coming to school;

- there are high-quality learning outcomes for all students;
- curriculum and learning pedagogy are seen as areas of change and development and not set in stone;
- collaborative cultures are established within the school and between neighbouring schools where staff share success and failures and learn from others;
- students see school as a learning centre and want to come to the building outside traditional hours;
- individuals in the school take responsibility for their roles – they take decisions rather have decisions forced on them;
- learning outcomes as measured by test scores improve slowly and consistently as deep learning improves the way staff and students work at learning challenges.

The point made earlier in the book about strategic conversations is important here. These conversations provide the framework of what a strategically focused school would look like and how it would 'feel' to work there. It is possible to build deep-seated strategic change and develop a culture of achievement in the school, which values wider learning outcomes as well as delivering short-term outcomes on the way. The starting point on the journey should not be the short-term results but the strategic change objectives and what they would look like in terms of measures of strategic success. In Steven Covey's (1989: 95) words: 'Begin with the end in mind.'

Be morally driven

Strategically focused schools must be based on values and beliefs, they must be morally driven. The analogy is that they need a moral compass for direction as well as a rudder for steering towards that direction. The central question of education may be: 'Education for what?' This query elicits a number of responses such as: education for the individual's own development, education for employability or education for citizenship, but underpinning these and other definitions is the concept of education as part of a moral purpose. The basic premise is that an educated society and an educated person is a 'good' thing. 'Good' in this sense can be seen in terms of education developing knowledge and understanding, and enabling the individual to see their personal situation and development in the context of others. In an interdependent society, the rights of individuals are balanced by their responsibilities to others in that society.

Education should be framed in terms of improving both the individual's and society's potential to improve in a sustainable and ethical way. This is dependent, as we saw in Chapter 3, on the values and beliefs that are held in the school. One of the roles of the educational leader is that of articulating the moral purpose of the school and the place of values in the strategic journey. While improving examination results over the long term is beneficial as an outcome for the school, it must be part of improving the understanding of deep learning and learning as part of a lifelong approach. Clear strategic objectives need to be set to define how the school will improve both the lives of individual children and their community.

Leaders also need to be morally driven in the choices they make and the role model they provide. Leaders make choices about how their schools make choices, and about how they interact on a number of issues. Let us have a look at some of these. Recently I was part of a discussion with primary school headteachers about Key Stage 2 results. The way that the testing regime affects schools is also a moral issue. One headteacher complained that one school in its neighbourhood with a one-form entry intake always achieved a 100 per cent in the English and Maths results every year. How do they do that? One possibility is that over a five-year period they admit only able children and no one with special needs ever comes to the school! Another is that they are creative with the way they administer and run the tests! Yet another is that they spend the whole of year 6 cramming for the test! It would seem that a school serving a normal catchment area poses moral questions about its 100 per cent results as much as the school that is consistently underachieving. I would suspect the local education authority (LEA) and the DfES may see it 'morally' unacceptable for a school consistently to underperform against its benchmarks. Indeed they do, and a variety of intervention measures and Ofsted categories await those who consistently underperform. However, I doubt if the moral basis of always achieving 100 per cent is ever questioned!

The way that leaders develop deep sustainable learning as the priority and see short-term tests as checks on that road is critical. The danger is to abandon deep-learning approaches and corrupt the whole curriculum process to achieve marginally higher results. These are profound moral issues. In setting the direction of the school, the way that leaders interpret externally imposed requirements is a moral and a curricular issue about the purpose of education. Obeying orders 'from on high' to the detriment of children is a moral choice! In discussions, leaders often use the leadership mantra approach and ask 'What is in the best interests of the children?' to determine what moral stance to take. Establishing a value system and set of beliefs for the school provides the moral template on which to judge current and future decisions and the direction of the school. The way that leaders undertake their strategic role and provide a moral role model is a key factor in the school. The school should move beyond being functionally competent and seek to provide, in new and diverse ways, opportunities for all its children. In doing so, it needs to be a moral community that operates in a way that benefits its own children and staff but does not do so to the detriment of others. The moral challenge for leaders is obviously to challenge poor performance but it is sometimes even more difficult to challenge satisfactory performance and try to achieve excellence. Often, cruising or strolling schools lack the moral leadership to go one step better; they lack the moral leadership to seek the best. Strategically focused schools have this leadership as they are always striving to improve.

Starratt (2005) in his account of 'Ethical leadership' provides a compelling case for those reflecting on the ethical base that guides the moral leadership of schools. He sees the role of the individual leader in a school comprising the role of an individual human being, as a citizen, as a teacher and as an educational leader. The way that individuals behave and model behaviour for others in each of these four roles is crucial for moral leadership. Personal integrity leads to a responsibility for the integrity of the curriculum, the integrity of learning and the integrity of citizenship. Starratt sees the moral processes and outcomes displayed by educational leaders as authentic relationships which cultivate learning, teaching and democratic stewardship of the school community.

The two foci of morally driven schools, when taking a strategic perspective, are based on the answer not only to the question 'What do you want to be in the future?' but also 'Why do you want to be that in the future?' The 'what' question concerns the skills and talents that individuals develop and the role that they will play. The 'why' question should be based on the contribution or difference an individual can make to the wider good of society and not just his or her personal well-being. Schools are a little like monasteries in the 'Dark Ages' where writing and literature and faith were kept alive in a complex and confusing time. In an increasingly materialistic self-orientated world, a school is one of the few centres of moral certainty and values. This role should not be underestimated.

The way to move forward is not based on a list of functional achievements but achievements that contribute to new educational understandings, new tolerance and new ways of supporting community and individuals. In short, strategically focused schools seek educational aims that morally enhance the world in which the school exists.

Focus on learning

One of the key characteristics of strategy is that it makes organizations focus on the core purpose of their activities and how these purposes can be developed in the future. The one overriding focus of a school is learning. Reasserting this core purpose is essential if learning is not to be subsumed in a series of other factors in the planning process. When we discuss learning we need to concentrate on the learning of the children in the care of the school. This is not just confined to the academic sphere; successful learning can be seen in how children achieve academically, socially, spiritually, physically and emotionally; it is children 'being all they can be'. However, learning should not be seen as something that we 'do to children'. Rather it should be the central cultural and organizational ethos of the school. How adults in the school learn, and how they develop a reflective learning culture, and how the school becomes a 'learning organization', are essential if the totality of learning is to be the central feature of the school.

The nature of learning poses a major strategic challenge to schools because of the attributes of short-term accountability and standards frameworks. If we were to think of learning as moving from shallow learning to complex learning and then to deep learning we could characterize this as follows:

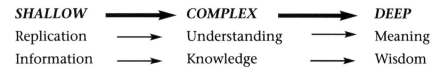

SHALLOW		*COMPLEX*		*DEEP*
Replication	→	Understanding	→	Meaning
Information	→	Knowledge	→	Wisdom

The challenge for schools is that the short-term accountability demands tend to require the replication of information with some attributes of complex learning, but assess little of the learning on the complex to deep end of the spectrum. Sustainable learning requires that we develop in children both the love of learning itself and some understanding of the meaning of complex knowledge so they can exercise wisdom to make informed choices in their lives. This links strongly to moral leadership in preserving the integrity of the teaching and learning process, while it has to ensure that external accountability does not corrupt its process and develop an approach which is merely teaching to the tests. We looked earlier at strategic measures of success. If, five years after leaving school, an individual was an avid reader and a participant in healthy exercise, that may be a better assessment of deep learning in the English and physical education lessons that they undertook than the results of the end-of-stage tests they may have taken in those subjects while at school. The key focus of a strategically focused school needs to be on developing complex and deep learning that provides an education that sustains children on their life's journey.

A similar approach needs to be adopted by adults in the school community. The title of headteacher or school principal should possibly be replaced by the term 'lead learner'. The importance for adults to recognize that, although they have existing skills, knowledge and qualifications, they are on a learning journey and not at its end, is vital. There is a significant difference between universities in the UK and the USA when students complete their degree courses. In the UK students attend a graduation ceremony signalling the completion of a learning journey, while in the USA students attend a commencement ceremony signalling they are commencing their next learning journey. This is the view of adult learning we need to adopt in schools. Sadly there are staff who have views like 'Why do we need to go and visit other schools – what can we learn from them?' or 'We have excellent results – why do we need to look at new ways of doing things?' Fortunately, they are in the minority; strategically focused schools are constantly reassessing and challenging what they are doing about learning, both from reflection on internal experience, and exposure to new knowledge and experience from outside the school. Building strategic capability and capacity in the schools is creating a culture within the school, where the teachers and learning support staff are themselves continuously engaged in learning in the pedagogical and knowledge fields. Organizationally one of the significant challenges for school leaders is to construct time and space for reflection and reinterpretation of knowledge and experience, so that professional learning groups in the school can engage in dialogue to build new understandings and direction.

Lessons from the NCSL study, report fascinating leadership stories of how schools embed learning into the centre of their activities. The two case studies in Chapter 10 showed how leading headteachers prioritize research and development as a key part of their organizational design, as a means of creating impetus for learning development in their schools. We have also considered in this book the use of leadership mantras as a means of conveying values in simple but profound statements. The learning mantra might obviously be the one that most parents ask their child on returning from school 'What have you learnt at school today'. This could equally be the question that school leaders ask of their staff as a strategic conversation opener to focus on teachers' and learning assistants' personal and professional learning. Another favourite mantra is 'What difference have you made to children's learning today?' rather than asking: 'What have you taught today?'

Learning is also clearly associated with assessment. I am reminded of a story told to me by my good friend Professor John Novak. It concerns American baseball where the umpire has to call whether when the ball is pitched it is a strike or not. The first judge recalls that he has no problem in assessing whether the ball is in or out, he can call the strike without any problem. The second umpire says it is very difficult as the ball is travelling so fast all he can do is make the best judgement he can and call it a strike or not. The third umpire says 'It's nothing until I call it'. The message is that we make judgements about children's learning, often based on shallow knowledge tests, which have profound effects on their self-esteem and motivation. Calling a child average or poor or outstanding is not what strategically focused schools should be doing in terms of labelling children. Diagnostic information that contributes to the learning journey is a far more powerful contribution to the individual's educational potential. Strategically focused schools put learning at the centre of their agenda and use assessment as diagnostic: as assessment for learning and not of learning.

Pay attention to strategic processes

This book has devoted Chapters 4 to 7 to consider strategic processes. Why is this idea of processes so important? As I mentioned earlier, John Novak from Canada, in his work on invitational leadership, contrasts the 'done with' approach to the 'done to' approach which often leaves the staff 'done in'. In a democratic society participation at the workplace is a democratic value and working with people is indeed a morally good thing to do. The reason that strategically focused schools spend a great deal of time and effort on processes to involve staff is that it may be a morally right democratic approach, but it is also an organizationally effective thing to do because involvement:

- allows a wider range of talented people to contribute;
- draws on expertise and experience;
- builds consensus and agreement;
- builds transparency and understanding;
- articulates challenges and invites solutions.

Schools are living systems made up of people who can choose to contribute or not contribute, or choose to be positive to change or negative to change. Which choices they take can be influenced by the strategic leaders in the school. Ideally, you want all staff to be committed and enthusiastic, and indeed that may be the case in some schools. In others, leaders build capacity where increasing numbers of staff involve themselves in the articulation of the hopes and visions of the school and seek ways they can contribute. What is needed is a 'tipping point' when the critical number provide the impetus for strategic change. I was told by a new headteacher that on arriving at his school on the first day and meeting all the teaching staff he had a mental model of the staff's willingness to engage in dialogue and make the radical strategic changes the school needed. The model was this: 'It was like there was a crowd of staff around the school pond. Seven stood on the edge and three were in the pond splashing the others.' I said presumably you needed to get the three out? He said, 'absolutely not – the priority was to stop any more jumping into the pond!' Strategic change takes time and effort and leaders often report to me that they underestimate the time and effort needed. The approach should be to work with the willing (the seven) to start the strategic conversations, build ideas and visions, and then slowly draw the reluctant members on the staff to join in. If we start with the premise that everyone needs to be convinced and on side before we attempt the journey, it is unlikely in many schools the journey would ever begin.

The overwhelming evidence from the NCSL research project was that successful strategically focused schools were vibrant places where strategic conversations flourished. Reflecting on good practice, and seeking ideas about future practice and ways of rethinking education, were built into the way the school operated. This did not happen by chance; leaders in the school saw this as one of their major tasks. Leading and learning went together, so that new ideas had to be shared and validated by colleagues, to build a coherent view of which were important and significant, and that is where they were going to spend their time and effort. The processes that schools set up to reflect on experience honestly, in the absence of a blame culture, and to seek new ways of doing things, is the culture that needs to be enhanced in schools. Whether the formal strategic conversations that take place in meetings or development days or the informal ones that take place in the staffroom or the corridor, it is the outward looking dialogue that is paramount.

The culture of being open or closed to new ideas, and being aware or unaware of major educational and economic developments, is key for strategically focused schools to develop. This is amusingly represented by Robertson and Abbey (2001) who depict individuals in an organization as in Figure 11.2.

The purpose of strategic conversations is to increase awareness so there is a migration to the top half of the diagram in Figure 11.2 by the unaware as they become more aware. Similarly, we need to stimulate debate and discussion, so that more staff become involved in discussing the future of the school and by doing so move to the right of the diagram to the open-minded participant. Amusingly it might be said the aim of strategically focused schools is to develop more owls, cull the foxes and develop the rest! It might be a useful exercise if the reader were to consider if you have any of these 'animal' types on your staff, and significantly, what your plans are for them!

People, in terms of staff and students are our most valuable resource. How we enhance and develop this resource is the critical role of school leadership. Earlier in the book I say that that how we do something is as important as what we do for its success. The how is dependent on the processes that the strategically focused school establishes. This establishment must be followed by development and renewal if the school is to continue to move forward. Drawing up strategic frameworks and plans can only be considered to be the design stage of the process. If the plans are to be implemented, and make a difference to the direction of the school, they need to be embraced and acted upon by those who work in the school.

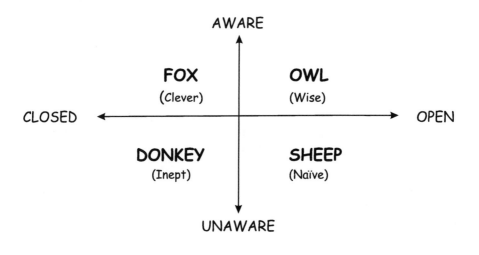

Figure 11.2 *People in organizations (Robertson and Abbey, 2002: 127)*

Compliance can achieve only a limited amount; what is far more important is commitment. Realizing that strategic conversations lead to participation and motivation, and are critical in achieving strategic capability, becomes the core activity of strategically focused schools. Strategic processes can be considered to be successful only when the staff no longer refer to the plans in the headteacher's office but start a dialogue about where the school is going and why it is going in that direction.

Pay attention to strategic approaches

Strategy, as we saw earlier, is too readily associated with just one strategic approach – that of strategic planning. There is a great danger in trying to predict and plan in too great detail and too far in advance. While, as we have seen, there are some actions or functions that lend themselves to a predictable linear approach. The danger is that this one approach dominates our thinking as the only way of doing anything. It is not clear, when President John Kennedy said in 1961 that the USA was going to land a man on the moon, that he actually had a plan to do it, or when Martin Luther King gave his 'I have a dream' speech, that he had a detailed schedule of how to achieve it. What they did have was a sense of direction and purpose and a determination to move forward. We need to combine in our leadership teams in schools the ability to move away from current paradigms and think creatively about alternative futures and future options. We need approaches in schools that can combine planning for what we know and realizing creativity to imagine alternatives and new state of operation.

There is a maxim that creative breakthroughs are 99 per cent perspiration and 1 per cent inspiration. The secret to success is providing the climate and framework that will support the 1 per cent and encourage it to happen. This book has put forward the idea that a strategically focused school needs to adopt a portfolio of strategic approaches. It also needs to create an infrastructure within the school to support those strategic approaches. It is relatively straightforward to set up an annual planning cycle linked to the budgetary cycle. Here short-term annual plans can be costed but also viewed in a medium- to longer-term planning context. The rational strategic plan is the organizationally least challenging as it deals with a set of known objectives and a set of predictable stages to proceed through to completion. It deals with the predictable, less creative side of the organization.

The challenge for leaders is to change the organizational climate to deal with emergent strategy and strategic intent. The reason to pay attention to these is that they offer opportunities for creativity and advancement. The precondition for emergent strategy is learning, and very often learning from mistakes! Are the staff in the school able to rationalize what has happened and look for solutions, or are they in a culture of blame and attributing mistakes to individuals? Reflection in learning organizations should be solution focused and forward-looking. The ability to learn and move on is as much about organizational culture as it is about the technical stages of the emergent strategy process.

Building a mind-set within a school of setting 'outrageous goals' and framing them in terms of strategic intents is a very powerful tool in schools transforming themselves and making strategic leaps to new levels of performance. Strategic intent is a liberating approach, if you can enable staff to move away from the obsession with detailed step-by-step planning. As one of the leaders in the NCSL study so eloquently put it: 'I had to get them to stop thinking about "but you can't go there because you need the route". The intents are established first because I think you don't make the big leaps if you have to know every little step on the way before you start.' Thinking of 'what can be' rather than 'what is too difficult' is a considerable shift in the organizational mind-set. The literature on strategic intent often talks about 'leveraging up' the organization to reach new levels of performance. The analogy given is the effort on a tyre lever which can have a profound effect through the forces of the lever. Thus setting intents can release forces in the school for considerable achievement. Strategic intent is a liberating concept because it focuses on profound educational changes that can revolutionize the way we do things, and does not get bogged down in the minute detail of planning at the initial stage. It should enable individuals to imagine and be creative – to be in fact 'right-brained' thinkers.

This does not happen by chance; the 1 per cent creativity needs to be nurtured in a system that debates, through strategic conversations, what are the intents the school is setting itself and how can it build a framework to do so. Or should we say we need to establish systems where the 99 per cent can happen so the 1 per cent can emerge? When we talk about strategic capability and capacity it refers to this ability within the school to build and create the dialogue to form the strategic intents. It also demands a learning capacity to engage proactively in building the means to turn ideas into reality; to link process through the appropriate approaches. Structuring learning opportunities and structuring dialogue and exposing staff to new ideas is something that strategic leaders can be proactive about.

The challenge in organizations such as schools is not to become overreliant on one planning approach. There may be a predominant approach at any one time but this can create problems. Clearly there is such a thing as an organizational life cycle. At some stage of a school's development there may be a rational planning part where clear direction is possible. There may be other times when consolidation and taking stock is the appropriate response. However, at others rapid change and the need to implant imposed policies mean that an emergent approach, with the ability for rapid reflection and absorption of lessons learned, needs to take place. Clearly the power of strategic intent is that it provides a backcloth of key substantial development that can take place while the more immediate demands of strategy can be met. The reason to pay attention to strategic approaches is that strategic leaders need to be adjusting the reliance on different strategic approaches as strategic contexts change. It is essential that leaders should always consider a portfolio of approaches rather than a single approach, to maximize organizational creativity and development.

Be part of a networked system

The task of leading and managing a school has become inherently more complex over the past two decades and more. Increased challenges in terms of expectations of schools, accountability demands and the nature of the broader society and economy have all impacted on school leadership. How to make sense of the shifting realities of schools and how they need to develop in the future is an awesome task. Simple relationships between central and local government and schools have been replaced by a system of interweaving relationships. Seeing schools as complex adaptive systems is one way of making sense of this complexity. How does an individual leader or group of leaders in a school draw down from this complex system the information and insights that it requires to understand its current and its developmental need? The solution that strategically focused schools need to adopt is a broad system of networks to draw on both to provide information but also to provide collegial support.

The three questions that schools need to answer when facing the challenge of gaining information to plot their future course are:

- What do we need to know?
- What do we currently know?
- How do we find out the information to close the gap between required knowledge and current knowledge?

Traditional linear relationships and reporting channels from the DfES and local education authorities have been rapidly supplemented by a plethora of quasi government and independent educational agencies ranging from Ofsted to the NCSL and professional associations. This process has been taken to a higher degree of complexity with the advent of multiple sources of information and relationships afforded by the World Wide Web and other electronic information linkage and exchange relationships. Individual leaders can now share with their colleagues at home and overseas an ever-increasing resource and dialogue regarding schools and their learning and organizational processes. What are the purposes of networking? It is useful to use the four 'I's to analyse this question. These are:

- Informing;
- Interpreting;
- Improving;
- Innovating.

Networking widens the scope of *information* available to leaders to make their decisions. The set of formal sources can be supplemented by a personal collegial network. Such personal networks should be local, regional, national and international to provide different perspectives on problems and challenges. In particular, personal and professional collegial links provide access to other leaders' thinking that will move the information stage into *interpretation* as other insights and perspectives are sought. The sharing of understanding on complex issues from a wider and different perspective can be a powerful means of handling strategic change. The purpose of this is, of course, to *improve* on current practice by sharing ideas and lessons learnt in individual schools. Incremental change is by definition slow and steady but a process of learning from others' experiences, good and bad, can significantly shorten the implementation time. This sharing of insights and interpretation is very significant when considering more radical *innovation* and *change*. In this case where the school's own experience is of little use, a broader set of ideas and experiences are invaluable.

Leaders I have worked with such as Derek Wise and Richard Wallis are constantly interacting with ideas from colleagues from home and overseas, to reframe their current practice, and to reflect on the future direction and developments in their school. They use their extensive networks to both develop new ideas and directions and to refine and develop existing practice. The formal networking opportunities through the Networked Learning Communities of the NCSL, the international visits programme of the British Council, NCSL and the Specialist Schools and Academies Trust, provide facilitated entry to leaders who wish to expand their networking abilities. These are opportunities that provide initial insights and solutions, but they also provide vehicles to develop sustainable strategic links for the long-term benefit of the school.

When talking to the leaders of strategically focused schools, they are outward looking and inclusive. They see the purpose of collaboration and sharing so that working smarter not harder may both improve what they do and do it in a sustainable way. A school trying to invent every new strategy, rather than learning from others and sharing development and expertise, offers little hope for long-term strategic improvement of the school. Seeking the best ideas from a wide range of sources provides a stimulus to embrace new ideas and change mind-sets. Innovative leaders not only do this themselves but they develop this sharing of proactive and exploring new ideas throughout the school. David Carter, one of the leading headteachers I have been privileged to work with, has set up exchanges with schools overseas where reciprocal hosting and holiday time visits have reduced the cost of sending significant numbers of his staff to a partner school in the USA to the cost of an airfare, which is little more expensive than a training course in London for the day! This is a major opportunity to have a significant number of staff, over a five-year period, develop an international perspective on educational change and development. Barbara Davies links her primary school with a school in Melbourne and one in Los Angeles to facilitate an international learning community. Staff work on joint projects for children, joint staff development activities and visits. This is an outstanding example of broadening the horizon of learning and development in the school.

Strategies for developing and extending networks are effective ways of developing strategic capacity throughout the school. Sustainability is not the same as maintainability. To recall the earlier definition of sustainability concerning continuous improvement without detrimental cost to the organization and community, networking is one approach to drawing in a wider set of ideas and solutions which do not exhaust the school through developing everything itself. The era of competition between schools in the UK is being challenged by an attempt to foster greater collaboration between schools. If leaders saw their responsibility to support and develop educational provision for schools in their area as part of a network of providers, rather than a set of competitors, then local networks may start to attack some of the more difficult educational challenges we face. Networking is beneficial at a national and international level but it can also be a powerful tool locally.

Develop sustainable strategic leadership across the school

In Chapter 2 consideration was given to the work of Collins and Porras (1994: 2) who studied firms who had been strategically successful over a long period of time. Two of their six factors relating to successful organizations concerned leadership: (1) they do not depend on a single visionary leader and (2) they grow their own leadership. This is a powerful starting point for reflecting on one of the factors to which strategically focused schools need to pay attention. This is the need to develop strategic leadership across a wider range of individuals in the school, in such a way that it is a powerful driver of strategic change, and that such dispersed ability is sustainable over the longer term. Individual strategic leaders, as we have seen in Chapter 9, prioritize their own leadership development. Reflecting on how skilful they are at accomplishing 'what strategic leaders do' and how far they match 'the characteristics strategic leaders possess', that were outlined in Chapter 9, is a useful starting point for a leadership developmental debate. Moving on from the individual stage, the developmental agenda needs to prioritize how the strategic leadership factors, again outlined in Chapter 9, can be developed in others.

Traditional views of school organization where headteachers provide the leadership, and middle managers administer curriculum area have changed radically to a model of distributed leadership over the last decade. A powerful mental model of headteachers of schools is that instead of seeing themselves as leaders of curriculum they should see themselves as *leaders of educational leaders*. Seeing the leadership function at all levels in the school is a developmental aim of strategically focused schools. This does not mean that the headteacher shares every leadership function with others in the school. Rather it purports to develop a leadership perspective and responsibility at different levels and parts of the school.

Classroom leaders have responsibility for their class and the development of curriculum and pedagogy. To do this they need to set the context of their day-to-day work in the wider context of the school's development and external developments. The significance of Chapters 4 to 7 that focused on strategic processes was to build strategic capacity through greater participation and involvement in building the strategic direction of the school. All those involved in the school should be encouraged to see the 'bigger picture' and where the school is going.

To have an effective strategic framework, the school will of course have strategic documentation. However, the true test of being strategically focused is that the concepts and ideas of the major strategic developments in the school should be part of the language and consciousness of teachers working in the school. Key to this process is not just understanding what is happening to a particular group of children this week or this term, but to see that in the context of the longer-term development of the child. Thus the coherence and progression is of utmost critical importance. This focuses on how what an individual teacher is doing contributes to the longer-term development of the child. This means reflecting on the school's need to adapt and change to meet future challenges by developing a strategic perspective to sit alongside the operational perspective. Comprehending, in strategic terms, where we have been and where we are going and providing an effective link is the core of strategic understanding.

Strategic leaders articulate the strategic purpose and direction of the school in formal staff training days as a means of re-emphasizing the direction of the school. They also do this in informal ways by the use of strategic conversations. The key to a sustainable, strategically focused school is that strategic conversations should also be part of the middle leaders' key interactions with colleagues in the school, as part of their leadership skills and ability. We saw in Chapter 7 that in articulating strategy as well as oral communication, how schools structure meetings and discussions is a key way of building an understanding of strategic purpose. This presents a challenge in schools, because curriculum co-ordinators and key stage co-ordinators in primary schools, and their counterpart heads of department and year in secondary schools are charged with the operational implementation of school plans. The key to successful leadership development is to support these leaders in creating the curriculum and learning discussions about the future direction of the school as well as the day-to-day issues. The need to develop a wider and longer-term perspective is the key developmental aim.

Attention has to be paid not only to developing strategic capacity and capability in the school, but also to make that capacity and capability sustainable in the longer term. The aim of strategically focused schools should be to have a succession planning policy in the school. Chapter 2 highlighted the Collins and Porras (1994) point about successful organizations developing their own leaders from within. This does not mean that the school never makes external appointments. What it does mean is that when appointments are made the developmental processes within the school are such that a credible internal candidate is in place and is appointable. For this to be the case such staff within the school must be able to undertake their own job effectively but also to understand the nature and dimensions of the senior post to which they aspire. Much progress has been made on this in recent years with schools developing initial in-house graduate training programmes, through to in-house management development courses including master's degrees. These need to become an increasing future of a recruitment and development package for staff.

The key resource that a school brings to the learning process of children is the quality of its teaching and learning support staff. They need constantly both to enhance their pedagogic skills and their wider contribution to the development of the school. By focusing on the strategic and leadership development needs, the school not only enhances its ability to be part of the wider development of the school but also develops its own leadership capacity and capability for the future. Strategically focused schools see this as a key development point.

Conclusion – whatever happened to Peter and Jane?

Jane continues her headship. She finds the job tiring and demanding but also exhilarating and challenging. She is restless, and always challenging current practice, but tries to balance her enthusiasm for change with the need to embed that change into sustainable practice in the school. Her core focus on learning has developed a learning culture based on strategic process and interaction between the staff. Developing staff and making extensive networks have helped her develop strategic leadership to a broader group of staff within the school. Her core moral focus remains 'What is in the best interest of the children?' She realizes there is much learning still to do and the strategic journey continues. Peter is now an Ofsted inspector!

References

Bartunek, J.M. and Necochea, R. (2000) 'Old insights and new times', *Journal of Management Inquiry*, 9(2): 103–13.

Baum, J.R., Locke, E.A. and Kirkpatrick, S.A. (1998) 'A longitudinal study of the relation of vision and vision communication to venture growth in entrepreneurial firms', *Journal of Applied Psychology*, 83(1): 43–54.

Beare, H., Caldwell, B.J. and Millikan, R.H. (1989) *Creating an Excellent School*. London: Routledge.

Bennett, D. (2000) *The School of the Future*. Nottingham: NCSL.

Bennis, W. and Nanus, B. (1985) *Leaders*. New York: Harper Row.

Boal, K.B. and Hooijberg, R. (2001) 'Strategic leadership research; moving on', *Leadership Quarterly*, 11(4): 515–49.

Boisot, M. (2003) 'Preparing for turbulence', in B. Garratt (ed.), *Developing Strategic Thought*. London: McGraw-Hill. pp. 29–63.

Bolman, L. and Deal, T.E. (1995) *Leading with Soul*. San Francisco, CA: Jossey-Bass.

Brubaker, D.L. (2005) 'The power of vision', in D.L. Brubaker and L.D. Colbe, *The Hidden Leader*. Thousand Oaks, CA: Corwin Press.

Brubaker, D.L. and Colbe, L.D. (2005) *The Hidden Leader*. Thousand Oaks, CA: Corwin Press.

Bush, T. and Glover, D. (2003) *School Leadership: Concepts and Evidence*. Nottingham: National College for School Leadership.

Campbell, A. and Yeung, S. (1990) 'Do you need a mission statement?' Ashridge Strategic Management Centre, Special Report No. 1208. London: Economist Publications.

Claxton, G. (2002) *Building Learning Power*. Bristol: TLO.

Coble, L.D. (2005) 'The power of learning', in D.L. Brubaker and L.D. Coble, *The Hidden Leader*. Thousand Oaks, CA: Corwin Press.

Collins, J. (2001) *Good to Great*. London: Random House Business Books.

Collins, J.C. and Porras, J.I. (1994) *Built to Last: Successful Habits of Visionary Companies*. New York: HarperCollins.

Covey, S. (1989). *The 7 Habits of Highly Effective People*. New York: Simon & Schuster.

Crianer, S. and Dearlove, D. (1998) *Gravey Training: Inside the Worlds Top Business Schools*. Oxford: Capstone.

Davies, B. (2003) 'Rethinking strategy and strategic leadership in schools', *Educational Management and Administration*, 31(3): 295–312.

Davies, B. (2007) *Developing Sustainable Leadership*. London: Sage.

Davies, B. and Davies, B.J. (2005) 'Strategic leadership' in B. Davies, (ed.) *The Essentials of School Leadership*. London: Paul Chapman Publishing.

Davies, B., Davies, B.J. and Ellison, L. (2005) *Success and Sustainability: Developing the Strategically Focused School*. Nottingham: National College for School Leadership.

Davies, B. and Ellison, L. (1999) *Strategic Direction and Development of the School*. London: Routledge.

Davies, B. and Ellison. L. (2003), *The New Strategic Direction and Development of the School*. London: Routledge.

Davies, B.J. (2004) 'An investigation into the development of a strategically focused primary school', EdD thesis, University of Hull.

Deal, T. and Peterson, K.D. (1999) *Shaping School Culture*. San Francisco, CA: Jossey Bass.

Freedman, M. (2003) *The Art and Discipline of Strategic Leadership*. New York: McGraw-Hill.

Fullan, M. (2004) *Leadership and Sustainability: System Thinkers in Action*. Thousand Oaks, CA: Corwin Press.

Gardner, H. (1985) *The Mind's New Science*. New York: Basic Books.

Garratt, B. (2003) *Developing Strategic Thought*. London: McGraw-Hill.

Gill, R. (2001) 'Beyond transformational leadership', paper presented at Bernard M. Bass Festschriff, Binghamton, New York.

Gratton, L. (2000) *Living Strategy: Putting People at the Heart of Corporate Purpose*. London: Financial Times – Prentice Hall.

Hamel, G. and Prahalad, C.K. (1994) *Competing for the Future*. Boston, MA: HBS Press.

Handy, C. (1990) The *Age of Unreason*. London: Arrow Books.

Handy, C. (1994) *The Empty Raincoat: Making Sense of the Future.* London: Hutchinson.

Hargreaves, A. (2005) *'Sustainable leadership'*, in B. Davies (ed.), *The Essentials of School Leadership.* London: Paul Chapman Publishing.

Hargreaves, A. and Fink, D. (2005) *Sustaining Leadership.* San Francisco, CA: Jossey Bass.

Hay Group Education (2004) *A Culture for Learning.* London: Hay Group Education.

Jeans, M. (1998) 'Bridging the s-curve gap', in A. Kakabadse, F. Nortier and N.B. Abramovici (eds), *Success in Sight.* London: International Thompson Business Press. pp. 123–39.

Josephson, M. (1990) *Making Ethical Decisions.* Marina Del Rey, CA: The Josephson Institute of Ethics.

Kaplan, R.S. and Norton, D.P. (1996) *The Balanced Scorecard.* Boston, MA: HBS Press.

Kaplan, R.S. and Norton, D.P. (2001) *The Strategy-Focused Organization.* Boston, MA: Harvard Business School Press.

Kouzes, J.M. and Posner, B.Z. (1999) *Encouraging the Heart: A Leader's Guide to Rewarding and Recognizing Others.* San Francisco, CA: Jossey Bass.

Landsberg, M. (2003) *The Tools of Leadership.* London: HarperCollins.

MacBeath, J. (2004) *'Leadership'*, paper presented at the Second International Summit for Leadership in Education, Boston College, Boston, MA.

MacGilchrist, B., Myers, K. and Reed, J. (2004) *The Intelligent School.* London: Sage.

Marsh, D. (2000) 'Educational leadership for the twenty-first century – integrating three essential perspectives', in *The Jossey-Bass Reader on Educational Leadership.* San Francisco, CA: Jossey-Bass. pp.126–45.

Mintzberg, H. (1989) *Mintzberg on Management.* New York: Free Press.

Mintzberg, H. (2003) 'Strategic thinking as seeing', in B. Garrat (ed.), *Developing Strategic Thought.* London: McGraw-Hill.

Nanus, B. (1992) *Visionary Leadership.* San Francisco, CA: Jossey-Bass.

Novak. J. (2002) *Inviting Educational Leadership.* London: Pearson Education.

Ott, J.S. (1989) *The Organizational Culture Perspective.* Pacific Grove, CA: Brooks/Cole.

Parikh, J. (1994) *Intuition – The New Frontier of Management.* Oxford: Blackwell.

Prahalad, C.K. and Hamel, G. (1990) 'The core competencies of the corporation', *Harvard Business Review*, 68: 79–93.

Perkins, D, (2003) *King Arthur's Roundtable.* New York: Wiley.

Pfeffer, J. and Sutton, R. (2002) *The Knowing-doing Gap: How Smart Companies Turn Knowledge into Action.* Boston, MA: Harvard Business School Press.

Robertson, A. and Abbey, G. (2001) *Clued Up: Working Through Politics and Complexity.* London: Pearson Education.

Schön, D. (1987) *Educating the Reflective Practitioner.* San Francisco, CA: Jossey-Bass.

Smith, A. (1996) *Accelerated Learning in the Classroom*, Stafford: Network Press.

Stalk, G., Evans, P. and Schulman, L. (1992) 'Competing on capabilities: the new rules of corporate strategy', *Harvard Business Review*, 70(2): 57–69.

Starratt, R. (2005) 'Ethical leadership', in B. Davies (ed.), *The Essentials of School Leadership.* London: Paul Chapman Publishing.

Sternberg, R.J. (2002) 'Wisdom, schooling and society', keynote presentation to the 2002 International Thinking Skills Conference, Harrogate.

Tolkien, J.R.R. (1991) *The Lord of the Rings.* London: HarperCollins.

Van Der Heijden, K. (1996) *Scenarios – The Art of Strategic Conversation.* New York: Wiley.

Westley, F. and Mintzberg, H. (1990) 'Visionary leadership and strategic management', *Strategic Management Journal*, 10: 17.

Wilson, I. (1997) 'Focusing our organisations on the future: turning intelligence into action', *On the Horizon*, 5(3): 1–6.

Index

Added to a page number 'f' denotes a figure.